I0235979

NAVAL
POSTGRADUATE
SCHOOL

MONTEREY, CALIFORNIA

THESIS

ANALYSIS OF UNMANNED UNDERSEA VEHICLE (UUV) ARCHITECTURES AND AN ASSESSMENT OF UUV INTEGRATION INTO UNDERSEA APPLICATIONS

by

Daniel W. French

September 2010

Thesis Advisor:	John S. Osmundson
Second Reader:	James S. Griffin

Approved for public release; distribution is unlimited

THIS PAGE INTENTIONALLY LEFT BLANK

REPORT DOCUMENTATION PAGE		*Form Approved OMB No. 0704-0188*
Public reporting burden for this collection of information is estimated to average 1 hour per response, including the time for reviewing instruction, searching existing data sources, gathering and maintaining the data needed, and completing and reviewing the collection of information. Send comments regarding this burden estimate or any other aspect of this collection of information, including suggestions for reducing this burden, to Washington headquarters Services, Directorate for Information Operations and Reports, 1215 Jefferson Davis Highway, Suite 1204, Arlington, VA 22202-4302, and to the Office of Management and Budget, Paperwork Reduction Project (0704-0188) Washington DC 20503.		

1. AGENCY USE ONLY *(Leave blank)*	2. REPORT DATE September 2010	3. REPORT TYPE AND DATES COVERED Master's Thesis
4. TITLE AND SUBTITLE Analysis of Unmanned Undersea Vehicle (UUV) Architectures and an Assessment of UUV Integration into Undersea Applications		**5. FUNDING NUMBERS**
6. AUTHOR(S) Daniel W. French		
7. PERFORMING ORGANIZATION NAME(S) AND ADDRESS(ES) Naval Postgraduate School Monterey, CA 93943-5000		**8. PERFORMING ORGANIZATION REPORT NUMBER**
9. SPONSORING /MONITORING AGENCY NAME(S) AND ADDRESS(ES) N/A		**10. SPONSORING/MONITORING AGENCY REPORT NUMBER**
11. SUPPLEMENTARY NOTES The views expressed in this thesis are those of the author and do not reflect the official policy or position of the Department of Defense or the U.S. Government. IRB Protocol number _____.		
12a. DISTRIBUTION / AVAILABILITY STATEMENT Approved for public release; distribution is unlimited		**12b. DISTRIBUTION CODE**

13. ABSTRACT (maximum 200 words)

There are prominent unmanned undersea vehicle (UUV) systems existing in the commercial marketplace today, but these systems have a relatively small role and presence in U.S. Navy application. This thesis suggests what existing commercially available UUV system architectural attributes could be used *now* in U.S. Navy applications. After a survey of multiple existing commercial UUV systems, five of the prevalent systems in the marketplace were selected for analysis and comparison of their system architecture. This thesis included a comprehensive architectural analysis on seven specific architectural attributes of these UUV systems. Other UUV systems were also analyzed to support specific system architecture discussion. Major architecture considerations were made by the UUV system designers and likely drivers of existing system attributes were discussed as well as the benefits and disadvantages of these system attributes. Finally, based on the material and findings of the thesis, recommendations for a notional UUV system design and architecture for the U.S. Navy was presented.

14. SUBJECT TERMS unmanned undersea vehicle (UUV), autonomous undersea vehicle (AUV), system architecture, UUV survey, architectural attributes UUV recommendations for U.S Navy, UUV system analysis			**15. NUMBER OF PAGES** 149
			16. PRICE CODE

17. SECURITY CLASSIFICATION OF REPORT Unclassified	**18. SECURITY CLASSIFICATION OF THIS PAGE** Unclassified	**19. SECURITY CLASSIFICATION OF ABSTRACT** Unclassified	**20. LIMITATION OF ABSTRACT** UU

NSN 7540-01-280-5500

Standard Form 298 (Rev. 2-89)
Prescribed by ANSI Std. 239-18

i

THIS PAGE INTENTIONALLY LEFT BLANK

Approved for public release; distribution is unlimited

ANALYSIS OF UNMANNED UNDERSEA VEHICLE (UUV) ARCHITECTURES AND AN ASSESSMENT OF UUV INTEGRATION INTO UNDERSEA APPLICATIONS

Daniel W. French
Civilian, Department of the Navy
B.S., University of Rhode Island, 1987

Submitted in partial fulfillment of the
requirements for the degree of

MASTER OF SCIENCE IN SYSTEMS ENGINEERING

from the

NAVAL POSTGRADUATE SCHOOL
September 2010

Author: Daniel W. French

Approved by: John S. Osmundson
                Thesis Advisor

                James S. Griffin
                Second Reader

                Clifford Whitcomb
                Chairman, Department of Systems Engineering

THIS PAGE INTENTIONALLY LEFT BLANK

ABSTRACT

There are prominent unmanned undersea vehicle (UUV) systems existing in the commercial marketplace today, but these systems have a relatively small role and presence in U.S. Navy application. This thesis suggests what existing commercially available UUV system architectural attributes could be used *now* in U.S. Navy applications. After a survey of multiple existing commercial UUV systems, five of the prevalent systems in the marketplace are selected for analysis and comparison of their system architecture. This thesis includes a comprehensive architectural analysis on seven specific architectural attributes of these UUV systems. Other UUV systems were also analyzed to support specific system architecture discussion. Major architecture considerations are made by the UUV system designers and likely drivers of existing system attributes were discussed as well as the benefits and disadvantages of these system attributes. Finally, based on the material and findings of the thesis, recommendations for a notional UUV system design and architecture for the U.S. Navy are presented.

THIS PAGE INTENTIONALLY LEFT BLANK

TABLE OF CONTENTS

THIS PAGE INTENTIONALLY LEFT BLANK

LIST OF FIGURES

THIS PAGE INTENTIONALLY LEFT BLANK

LIST OF TABLES

THIS PAGE INTENTIONALLY LEFT BLANK

LIST OF ACRONYMS AND ABBREVIATIONS

ABS	Acrylonitrile Butadiene Styrene
ACDP	Acoustic Current Doppler Profiler
ACOMMS	Acoustic Communications
ARL	Applied Research Laboratory
ASW	Anti-Submarine Warfare
AUV	Autonomous Undersea Vehicle
AUVAC	Autonomous Undersea Vehicle Application Center
BOSS	Buried Object Scanning Sonar
BPAUV	Battlespace Preparation Autonomous Underwater Vehicle
CN3	Communications Navigation Network Node
CONOPS	Concept of Operations
CT&P	Conductivity, temperature and pressure
CTD	Conductivity, Temperature & Depth
DGPS	Differential Global Positioning System
DVL	Doppler Velocity Logger
EV	Electric Vehicle
FLS	Forward Look Sonar
GRP	Glass Reinforced Plastic
HDPE	High Density Polyethylene
HEV	Hybrid Electric Vehicle
IC	Internal Combustion
IEEE	Institute of Electrical and Electronics Engineers
IMU	Inertial Measurement Unit
INS	Inertial Navigation System
INU	Inertial Navigation Unit
IO	Information Operations
ISE	International Submarine Engineering
ISR	Intelligence, Surveillance and Reconnaissance
kW-Hr	Kilowatt-Hour
L&R	Launch and Recovery

LARS	Launch and Recovery System
LBL	Long Base Line
LDUUV	Large Displacement Unmanned Undersea Vehicle
LION	Lithium Ion
LPI	Low Probability of Intercept
m	Meter
MBE	Multi-Beam Echo-sounder
MCM	Mine Counter-Measures
N/A	Not Available
NAVCEANO	Naval Oceanographic Office
Ni-MH	Nickel Metal Hydride
NLW	Non-lethal weapons
PHEV	Plug-in Hybrid Electric Vehicle
REA	Rapid Environmental Assessment
REMUS	Remote Environmental Monitoring Units
RF	Radio Frequency
RMS	Remote Minehunting System
ROV	Remotely Operated Vehicle
SAS	Synthetic Aperture Sonar
SATCOM	Satellite Communications
SBP	Sub-Bottom Profiler
SLBL	Synthetic Long Baseline
SSS	Side Scan Sonar
TCS	Time Critical Strike
TRL	Technology Readiness Level
U.S.	United States
UHF	Ultra High Frequency
UN	United Nation
USBL	Ultra Short Baseline
UUV	Unmanned Undersea Vehicle
UUVMP	Unmanned Undersea Vehicle Master Plan
V	Volts

V^2	Velocity
W	Watts
W/Kg	Watts per Kilogram
WAAS	Wide Area Augmentation System
Wh/kg	Watt-Hours per Kilogram
Wh/L	Watt-Hours per Liter

THIS PAGE INTENTIONALLY LEFT BLANK

ACKNOWLEDGMENTS

I would like to express my gratitude and thanks to Ms. Elizabeth Wilson and Ms. Robin Silvia who helped organize and compile the UUV survey in Chapter II and also the references used in this research.

Lastly I would like to thank Ms. Janis Higginbotham for her much-needed assistance with formatting and final editing.

THIS PAGE INTENTIONALLY LEFT BLANK

I.   INTRODUCTION

A.   BACKGROUND

Over the past several decades, numerous unmanned undersea vehicle (UUV) systems have been developed, operated, marketed, produced, sold and utilized in-water for various purposes. The wide range of UUV systems varies from small to large over a number of varying form-factors, and are intended to conduct tasks such as oceanographic data measurements, bottom imagery, bathymetric imaging, collecting Intelligence, Surveillance and Reconnaissance (ISR), cable-laying, mine-detection, and many more. Existing UUV systems range from academic prototypes, government test-beds, commercial limited (small number) prototypes or production units to commercial, full-scale production units.   The spectrum of system maturity runs from relatively unproven laboratory single units to production vehicles that have logged thousands of at-sea operational hours. Figure 1 shows a UUV collage that attempts to capture the large scope of existing UUV systems.

These UUV systems have interesting and unique system architectural attributes that result from their operational environment, user requirements, and developed methods of deployment, recovery, tracking, command & control, navigation, providing energy, propulsion, sensing, special mission objectives and many more. Unmanned undersea vehicles have numerous common attributes, as well as many unique or custom characteristics. This thesis investigates these UUV architectures and discusses significant commonality, differences and drivers (i.e., operational environment and requirements) among them, and how they could be applied to military use.

UUVs have also been designed to be operated-from and integral-to some infrastructure as part of a concept of operations (CONOPs). How the UUV systems are deployed, controlled, data-harvested and recovered is a substantial driver to the UUV's system architecture. Operational infrastructures supporting the UUV CONOPs typically include assets and resources such as human operators, shore facilities, surface ships, submarines, satellite communications networks, and even aircraft. Various techniques

1

and UUV system architectural attributes have been developed to accommodate these various CONOPs, varying organizational cultures and infrastructures into which UUVs have been integrated. There is substantial commonality in commercial UUV systems in the market in this area. This study also investigates and discusses UUV infrastructure integration and CONOPs.

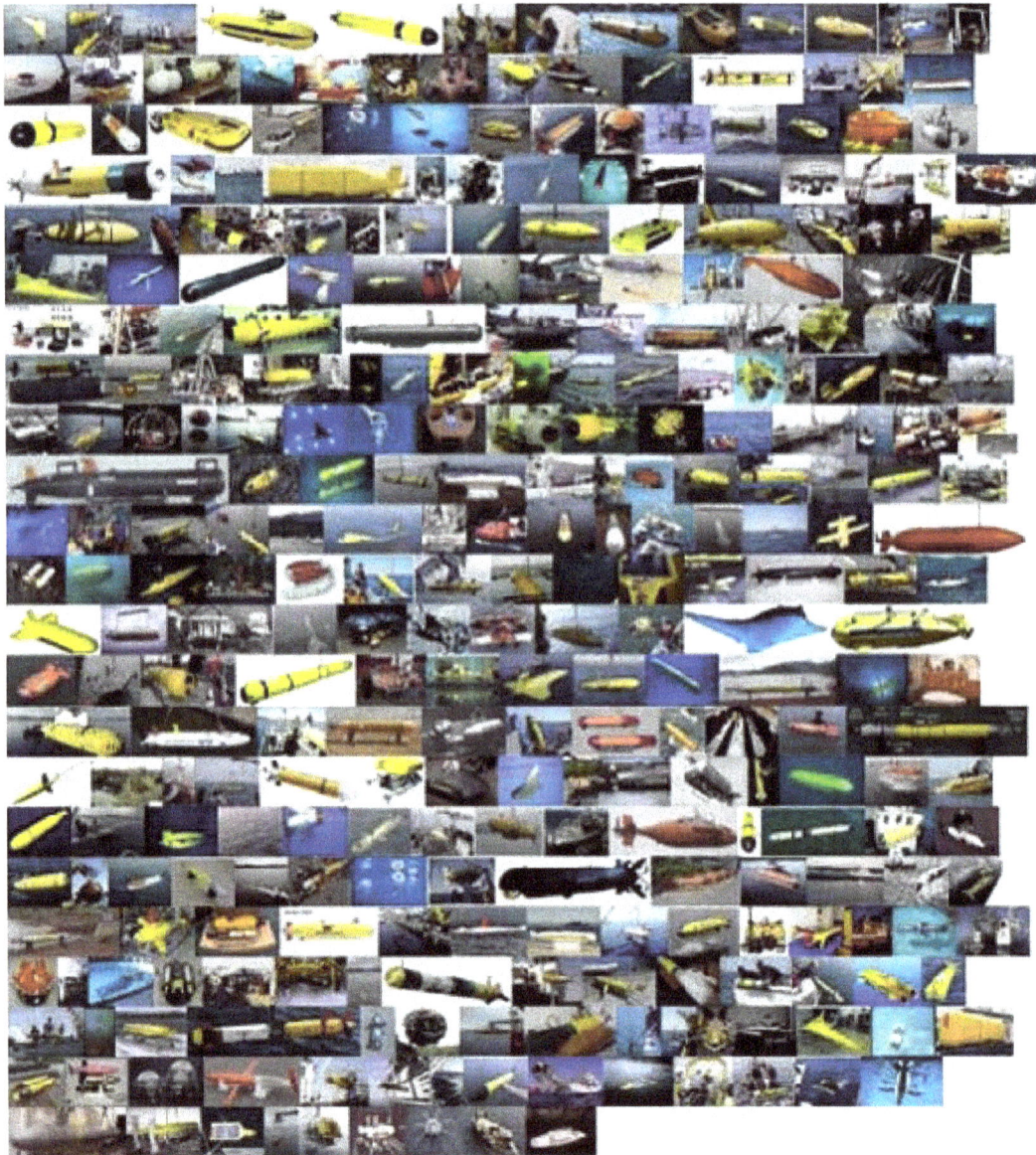

Figure 1. Various UUV Systems from fifty-one manufactures from Autonomous Undersea Vehicle Application Center (AUVAC) Web site [1].

The focus on UUV system architecture for this thesis is on commercial UUV systems and how commercial UUV systems integrate into the operational marketplace. How this existing integration could potentially be applied to Navy applications is also discussed. This study recommends vehicle-specific architectural attributes of commercial UUV systems that would be preferred for naval applications. Background is now provided on Navy plans for UUV systems, to help put military context to Navy UUV aspirations. The U.S. Navy published an Unmanned Undersea Vehicle Master Plan (UUVMP) in 2004 [2], where mission areas, UUV size classes, and enabling technologies were identified. Nine "sub-pillar" UUV mission areas, which were aligned with Sea Power 21 [3] Pillars (Sea Shield, Sea Base Sea Strike and ForceNet) for UUVs, in the UUVMP are:

UUV Mission Area Sub-Pillars in UUV Master Plan
1. Intelligence, Surveillance and Reconnaissance (ISR)
2. Mine Counter-Measures (MCM)
3. Anti-Submarine Warfare (ASW)
4. Inspection / Identification
5. Oceanography
6. Communications Navigation Network Node (CN3)
7. Payload Delivery
8. Information Operations (IO)
9. Time Critical Strike (TCS)

The UUVMP conducted a joint functional and mission analysis and a survey of existing Navy UUV infrastructure and designated four size (or displacement) classes for UUVs in the Navy to conform to: man-portable, lightweight vehicle, heavyweight vehicle and large. Figure 2 shows a compilation of UUVMP graphics and highlights Sea Power 21 Pillars, UUV Sub Pillars and UUV size classes.

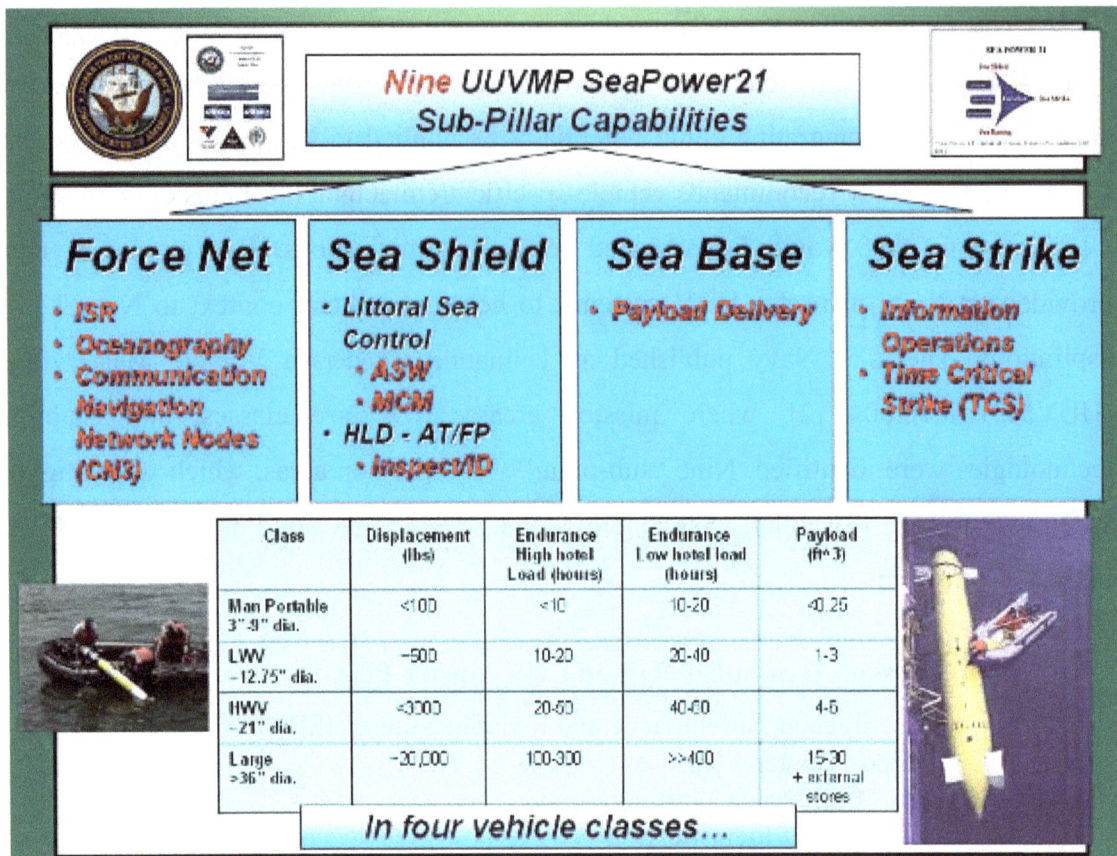

Figure 2. Compilation of UUV Master Plan graphics [2] illustrating Sea Power 21 Pillars, UUV "Linked" Sub Pillars and the four UUV vehicle classes.

Additionally, Navy vision in the UUVMP defined critical technologies that were important in multiple UUV mission sub-pillars. These technologies were considered low in maturity or low Technology Readiness Level (TRL) and are identified as:

1. Autonomy
2. Energy
3. Sensors / Processing
4. Networking / Low Probability of Intercept (LPI) Communications
5. Engagement / Intervention

While most are self-explanatory, the last technology area (engagement/intervention) refers to autonomous vehicle recovery, autonomous neutralizers, net extractions and non-lethal weapons (NLW). These technology areas, which the UUVMP identifies as critical and relatively "immature" technologically, are important areas that commercial UUV systems have been addressing with very specific architectural attributes and technical solutions. These technology areas and resulting solutions sets are evident in commercial UUV development and are discussed later.

B.   PURPOSE

The purpose of this study is to analyze the various system architectures of unmanned undersea vehicles (UUV), provide a comparative analysis of these UUV attributes, and recommend architectural features for Navy. The UUV attributes researched and discussed include: overall vehicle arrangement, form factor, propulsion, control surfaces, energy system, pressure hulls and wet volume, accommodations for sensors, communications, and launch and recovery.

C.   RESEARCH QUESTIONS

This thesis investigates UUV system architectures, how they compare, what drives architecture, and what commercial architectural attributes could be recommended for U.S. Navy use. The specific research questions are:

- How do architectures of different UUV systems compare?
- What are the major drivers and constraints for these architectural differences?
- What architectural similarities exist in a diverse product line of UUV systems?
- What architectural attributes are recommended for Navy use?

D.   BENEFITS OF STUDY

The thesis provides a relatively broad survey of commercially offered UUV systems and an analytical compilation of major UUV system architectural attributes for a sampling of these UUVs that are prevalent in the marketplace. Multiple UUV systems are now in operation, and were driven by commercial market demands (i.e., oil survey, oceanographic data collection, bathymetry, hydrography, etc...). This thesis provides a comprehensive understanding of what system architecture features are prominent and why they are prominent on UUVs. It provides the Navy with recommendations of what UUV system attributes should be leveraged for military applications.

E.   SCOPE AND METHODOLOGY

This thesis focuses on select commercially available UUV systems and their associated system architectural attributes. Five prominent UUV systems are analyzed for an understanding of their operational objectives, "deliverables" to customers, concepts of operations (CONOPs), architectural features and operating constraints. Additionally, other UUV systems that are not considered in "high production" are analyzed to support the architectural discussions and points in this study. These existing architectural features of UUVs have been driven by needs (requirements), user demand, constraints of CONOPs, and the operating environment. A comparison of these architectural features is included to capture contrasts and similarities of different UUV systems. After this basis of existing systems is created, architectural recommendations for Navy applications are offered from a system engineering perspective.

The methodology used to generate this thesis study consists of conducting UUV systems research, down-selecting commercial candidates for deeper analysis of system architecture, presenting a summary and analysis of UUV architectural features, and providing recommendations for possible U.S. Navy. The information obtained to support this effort is all open source information collected from journals, magazines, texts, Navy documents and UUV provider Web sites. A sequenced breakdown of this thesis methodology is as follows:

1.   Conduct a broad literature review of existing UUV systems and their architectures. Generate a survey of commercial UUV systems.

2.   Perform down-selection to more prominent UUV systems that are available. This would include commercial UUV systems that are actually manufactured in significant quantities that are considered representative of market demand.

3.   Analyze/research existing UUV system architectures of these UUVs. This would include analysis of architectural attributes such as hull form factors,

6

pressure hulls, propulsion techniques, sensors, navigation methods, communications and command and control.

4.   Provide recommendations of system architectural features of UUVs that the Navy should consider for its present and future use. This would include comparing existing architectures in terms of benefits and limiting factors and suggesting which architectural features are best from a system engineering perspective.

The next chapter consists of a broad survey of commercial UUV systems.

THIS PAGE INTENTIONALLY LEFT BLANK

II. SURVEY OF UUVS IN THE COMMERCIAL MARKETPLACE

A. INTRODUCTION

This chapter presents a survey of unmanned undersea vehicle (UUV) systems found and investigated on the Web. All data obtained was open source via product provider Web sites, brochures or published material from journals, magazines and texts. The commercial UUV survey presented in the next section was based on UUVs being commercially available for purchase by a provider. This survey does *not* include UUV systems from academia, Navy laboratories, strictly military use or systems that generally were not designed, presented or offered in potential quantity. Commercially available systems, available in the marketplace were considered good representations for the investigation of UUV system architecture. The UUV survey is a comprehensive compilation of commercial UUVs and forms a population of UUVs that was used as a selection set for further, more in-depth, architectural analysis (beginning in Chapter III).

B. SURVEY OF EXISTING COMMERCIALLY PRODUCED UUV SYSTEMS

Each commercial UUV system in the survey was put into a common quad-chart format with a title block that reflects UUV system name (or designation), country of origin, reference number and source for information for that particular UUV. The four quadrants consist of applications, features, energy/endurance/propulsion and payload/sensors. The information on each UUV chart was representative of what the UUV providers tended to highlight, what had relevance to an architecture discussion and simply what was common information amongst the UUV Web sites. Thirty-four commercial UUVs are presented in Figures 4 through 37. Figure 3 is a list of acronyms commonly used in the UUV quad charts.

- ACDP – Acoustic Current Doppler Profiler
- ASW – Anti Submarine Warfare
- BPAUV – Battlespace Preparation Autonomous Underwater Vehicle
- CTD – Conductivity, Temperature & Depth
- DGPS – Differential GPS
- DVL – Doppler Velocity Logger
- IMU – Inertial Measurement Unit
- INS – Inertial Navigation System
- INU – Inertial Navigation Unit
- ISR – Intelligence, Surveillance and Reconnaissance
- kW.hr – Kilowatts per Hour
- L & R – Launch and Recovery
- LBL – Long BaseLine
- Lion – Lithium Ion
- MCM – Mine Counter Measures
- REA – Rapid Environmental Assessment
- RMS – Remote Minehunting System
- SAS – Synthetic Aperture Sonar
- SLBL – Synthetic Long BaseLine
- USBL – Ultra Short BaseLine
- WAAS – Wide Area Augmentation System

Figure 3. Common acronyms in UUV survey quad-charts.

Country of Origin: Denmark

Atlas Maridan Seaotter MKII

Ref No: 1

Provider: Atlas Maridan

Source: www.maridan.atlas-elektronik.com

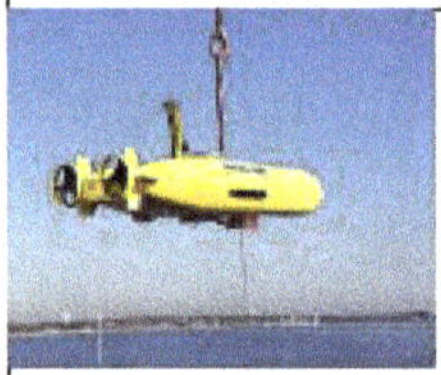

L & R: Stinger System from Ship

Applications

- Ocean Surveying
- Ocean Monitoring
- Ocean Sampling
- Pipe and Cable tracking/inspection

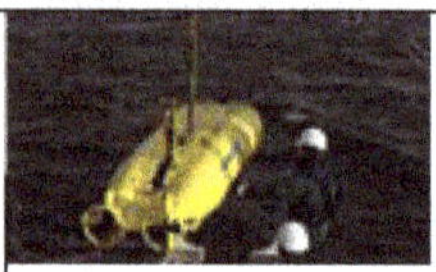

Length: 3.50 m

Width: .98m

Height: .48m

Features

Dry/Air Weight: <1,300kg

Depth Rating: 600m or 1,500m

Construction: Modular

IOC/Status:

Energy, Endurance & Propulsion

Energy System: Lithium Polymer

Energy Capacity:

Range/Endurance: 90 nm at 4 knots

Max Speed: 8 knots

Propulsion: Counter-rotating twin propellers

Payload and Sensors

Payload Capacity:

Communication:

Navigation: Aided Inertial Navigation System, Kalman filter, LBL, USBL, Synthetic LBL (SLBL) Control

Config/Actuators:

Sonars/Sensors: Side Scan, Sub bottom profiler, multi-beam echosounder, ADCP camera

Figure 4. UUV #1: Atlas Maridan Seaotter MKII

Country of Origin:	**Bluefin 9**		Ref No: 2
USA	Provider: Bluefin Robotics Corp	Source: www.bluefin.com	

	Applications		Features
			Dry/Air Weight: 50kg
			Depth Rating: 200m
		Length: 1.65m	Construction:
L & R: One Person Portable		Diam: .24m	IOC/Status:

Energy, Endurance & Propulsion	Payload and Sensors
Energy System: 1.5kW.hr Lion	Payload Capacity:
Energy Capacity:	Communication:
Range/Endurance: 12 hours nominal load	Navigation:
Max Speed: 2.06 meters per second	Config/Actuators:
Propulsion:	Sonars/Sensors: Side Scan Sonar, CTD

Figure 5. UUV #2: Bluefin-9

Country of Origin:	**Bluefin 12**		Ref No: 3
USA	Provider: Bluefin Robotics Corp	Source: www.bluefin.com	

	Applications		Features
	▪Harbor & Port Security		Dry/Air Weight: 250kg
	▪Hydrographic Survey		Depth Rating: 200m
		Length: 65inches	Construction: Modular
L & R:	▪Seabed Mapping	Diam: 12.75 in	IOC/Status:

Energy, Endurance & Propulsion	Payload and Sensors
	Payload Capacity:
Energy System:	Communication:
Energy Capacity: 4.5kW.hr	Navigation:
Range/Endurance:	Config/Actuators:
Max Speed: 2.57 meters per second	Sonars/Sensors:
Propulsion:	

Figure 6. UUV #3: Bluefin-12

11

Country of Origin: USA	Bluefin 21 BPAUV		Ref No: 4
Provider: Bluefin Robotics Corp		Source: www.bluefin.com	

Applications	Features
	Dry/Air Weight: 362.87 kg
	Depth Rating: 6,000m
Length: 130in	Construction:
Diam: 21 in	IOC/Status:
L & R:	

Energy, Endurance & Propulsion	Payload and Sensors
	Payload Capacity:
Energy System: 4.5kW.hr Lion	Communication:
Energy Capacity:	Navigation: AHRS, DVL,
Range/Endurance: 18 hours at 3 knots	Config/Actuators:
Max Speed: 2.06 meters per second	Sonars/Sensors: Side Scan Sonar
Propulsion:	

Figure 7.   UUV#4: Bluefin-21 BPAUV

Country of Origin: USA	Bluefin 21		Ref No: 5
Provider: Bluefin Robotics Corp		Source: www.bluefin.com	

Applications	Features
	Dry/Air Weight:
	Depth Rating: 6,000m
Length:	Construction:
Diam: 21 inches	IOC/Status:
L & R:	

Energy, Endurance & Propulsion	Payload and Sensors
	Payload Capacity:
Energy System:	Communication:
Energy Capacity:	Navigation:
Range/Endurance:	Config/Actuators:
Max Speed: 2.06 meters per second	Sonars/Sensors:
Propulsion:	

Figure 8.   UUV #5: Bluefin-21

Country of Origin:	Boeing Echo Ranger		Ref No: 6
USA	Provider: Oceaneering, Boeing & Fugro		Source: www.auvac.org

	Applications		Features
	•Cable Route Survey		Dry/Air Weight: 5,308kg
	•Oil and Gas Survey		Depth Rating: 3,050m
	•Pipeline Route Survey	Length: 5.5m	Construction: Modular
L & R: Crane or custom cradle	•Seabed Mapping	Width: 1.27m	IOC/Status: 2004
		Height: 1.27m	

Energy, Endurance & Propulsion	Payload and Sensors
Energy System:	Payload Capacity:
Energy Capacity:	Communication:
Range/Endurance:	Navigation:
Max Speed: 4 meters per second	Config/Actuators:
Propulsion:	Sonars/Sensors: Forward Look Sonar, Side Scan Sonar, Gap-Filler Sonar, Electro-Optical Identification Sensor

Figure 9.   UUV #6: Boeing Echo Ranger

Country of Origin:	ECA Alistar 3000		Ref No: 7
France	Provider: ECA Group		Source: www.eca.fr

	Applications		Features
	•Underwater Pipeline pre and post lay surveys		Dry/Air Weight: 2,300kg
			Depth Rating: 3,000m
	•Pipeline inspections	Length: 5,000mm	Construction:
L & R: From Ship	•Oil Rig Inspections	Width: 1,680mm	IOC/Status:
		Height: 1,450mm	

Energy, Endurance & Propulsion	Payload and Sensors
	Payload Capacity: 150kg
Energy System:	Communication: RF link, Acoustic modem, Acoustic localization transponder, GPS/DGPS receiver
Energy Capacity:	
Range/Endurance: 24 hours	Navigation: INS & Kalman Filter, DVL, Altimeter, Depth Sensor
Max Speed: >4 knots	
Propulsion:	Config/Actuators:
	Sonars/Sensors:Obstacle avoidance sonar, Side Scan Sonar, sub-bottom profiler, camera, Sound Velocity Prob

Figure 10.   UUV #7: ECA Alistar 3000

13

Country of Origin: France	ECA Alistar		Ref No: 8
Provider: ECA Group		Source: www.eca.fr	

Applications	Features	
▪Hydrography ▪Close support to task force (organic mine warfare) ▪Intelligence Gathering ▪MCM ▪Rapid Environmental Assessment (REA)	Length: 4,400mm to 5,000mm Width: 1,680mm Height: 1,450mm	Dry/Air Weight: 800 to 960kg Depth Rating: 300m Construction: IOC/Status:

Energy, Endurance & Propulsion	Payload and Sensors
Energy System: Energy Capacity: Range/Endurance: 12 – 20 hours Max Speed: >8 knots Propulsion: L & R: From Ship	Payload Capacity: Communication: RF link, Acoustic modem, Acoustic localization transponder, GPS/DGPS receiver, Navigation: INS, DVL, USBL, or LBL Config/Actuators: Sonars/Sensors: Obstacle avoidance sonar, Side Scan Sonar, Synthetic Aperture Sonar, sub-bottom profiler, video camera, CTD probe, acoustic camera

Figure 11.   UUV #8: ECA Alistar

Country of Origin: USA	Fetch 2		Ref No: 9
Provider: SIAS Patterson Inc		Source: www.auvac.com	

Applications	Features	
▪Mine Counter Measures (MCM) ▪Harbor and port security ▪Environmental Monitoring ▪Hull Inspection	Length: 1.96m Width: 0.29m Height: 0.29m	Dry/Air Weight: 73kg Depth Rating: 150 Construction: Fiberglass IOC/Status:

Energy, Endurance & Propulsion	Payload and Sensors
Energy System: Energy Capacity: Range/Endurance: Max Speed: 6.5 meters per second Propulsion: L & R: Two person portable	Payload Capacity: Communication: Navigation: Config/Actuators: Sonars/Sensors:

Figure 12.   UUV #9: Fetch 2

Country of Origin: USA	Fetch 3		Ref No: 10
Provider: SIAS Patterson Inc		Source: www.auvac.com	

Applications	Features
•Mine Counter Measures (MCM) •Harbor and port security •Environmental Monitoring •Hull Inspection	Dry/Air Weight: 98kg Depth Rating: 150m Length: 2.1m Construction: Width: 0.35m IOC/Status: Height: 0.35m

Energy, Endurance & Propulsion	Payload and Sensors
Energy System: Energy Capacity: Range/Endurance: Max Speed: 5 meters per second Propulsion: L & R: Two Person Portable	Payload Capacity: Communication: Navigation: Config/Actuators: Sonars/Sensors:

Figure 13.   UUV #10: Fetch 3

Country of Origin: Iceland	Gavia Defense		Ref No: 11
Provider: Hafmynd ehf		Source: www.gavia.is	

Applications	Features
•Search & Recovery •Port Security •Specialized Payloads & research L & R: Two person portable •Mine Counter Measures (MCM) • ASW training •Rapid Environmental Assessment (REA)	Dry/Air Weight: from 49kg Depth Rating: 500 or 1,000m Length: 1.8m for base vehicle (Typical MCM 2.6m) Construction: Modular Diam: 200mm IOC/Status: 1997

Energy, Endurance & Propulsion	Payload and Sensors
Energy System: 1.2 kW Lion rechargeable cells per module Energy Capacity: Range/Endurance: Typically around 7 hours with DVL INS, greater endurance when using acoustic positioning Max Speed: >5.5 knots Propulsion:	Payload Capacity: Communication: Wireless LAN, Iridium link, Acoustic modem, Navigation: GPS and Fluxgate Compass, optional DVL aided LBL Config/Actuators: Sonars/Sensors: Side Scan Sonar, camera, Obstacle Avoidance Sonar, Sound Velocity Meter, other configurations available

Figure 14.   UUV #11: Gavia Defense

15

Country of Origin: Iceland	Gavia Offshore Surveyor		Ref No: 12
	Provider: Hafmynd ehf	Source: www.gavia.is	

	Applications		Features
• Various construction support and inspection tasks for pipeline and platforms	▪Bathymetric Surveys ▪Environmental Surveys ▪Exploration	Length: 2.7m Diam: 200mm	Dry/Air Weight: 70-80 kg (typical depending on config) Depth Rating: 500 or 1,000m
L & R: Two Person Portable		IOC Status: 1997	Construction: Modular

Energy, Endurance & Propulsion	Payload and Sensors
Energy System: 1.2kW Lion rechargeable cells per module Energy Capacity: Range/Endurance: 4-5 hours typical at 3 knots per rechargeable battery module (vehicle can operate with two batteries for increased endurance) Max Speed: >5.5 knots Propulsion:	Payload Capacity: Communication: Wireless LAN, Irisium link, Acoustic modem Navigation: DGPS ready receiver, DVL Inertial Nav, Kearfott T-24 INS, Teledyne RDI DVL, direct sound velocity meter, other configurations available Config/Actuators: Sonars/Sensors: Depending on configuration

Figure 15.   UUV #12: Gavia Offshore Surveyor

Country of Origin: Iceland	Gavia Scientific		Ref No: 13
	Provider: Hafmynd ehf	Source: www.gavia.is	

	Applications		Features
▪Archeology, wreck finding & mapping ▪Water Column ▪3D CTD mapping	▪Oceanography ▪Limnology ▪Habitat assessment ▪Hydrography ▪Bathymetric Surveys	Length: 1.8 for base vehicle Diam: 200mm	Dry/Air Weight: From 49kg for base vehicle Depth Rating: 500 or 1,000m Construction: Modular IOC/Status: 1997

Energy, Endurance & Propulsion	Payload and Sensors
Energy System: 1.2kW Lion rechargeable cells per module Energy Capacity: Range/Endurance: Typically around 7 hours with DVL INS, greater when using acoustic positioning Max Speed: >5.5 knots Propulsion: L & R: Two Person Portable	Payload Capacity: Communication: Wireless LAN, Iridium link, Acoustic modem Navigation: GPS and Fluxgate compass, optional DVL aided INS, optional DVL aided LBL Control Config/Actuators: Sonars/Sensors: Depending on configuration

Figure 16.   UUV #13: Gavia Scientific

16

Country of Origin: Norway	Hugin 1000	Ref No: 14
	Provider: Kongsberg Gruppen	Source: www.km.kongsberg.com

	Applications	Features
	•Offshore surveying for oil and gas industry •Naval MCM & REA •Marine Research	Length: 4.5m (4.7m for 3,000m configuration) Diameter: 75cm IOC/Status: 1997	Dry/Air Weight: 650-850kg Depth Rating: 1,000 or 3,000m Construction: Modular – Carbon Fiber laminate material & Syntactic foam

Energy, Endurance & Propulsion	Payload and Sensors
Energy System: 15kW.hr LiPolymer Energy Capacity: Range/Endurance: 24hrs @ 4 knots (with MBE, SSS, SBP, and CTD) Max Speed: 6 knots Propulsion: L & R: Stinger based system for ship stern launch	Payload Capacity: Communication: Acoustic command, data links, RF, Iridium, Ethernet, WLAN Navigation: IMU, DVL, Depth, USBL, NavP TP Ranging, GPS, TerrNav Config/Actuators: Sonars/Sensors: Side Scan Sonar, Synthetic Aperture Sonar, Multibeam echo sounder, sub-bottom profiler, fishery sonar, laser plankton counter

Figure 17.   UUV #14: HUGIN 1000

Country of Origin: Norway	Hugin 3000	Ref No: 15
	Provider: Kongsberg Gruppen	Source: www.km.kongsberg.com

	Applications	Features
 L & R: Stinger based system	•Offshore surveying for oil and gas industry •Marine Research	Length: 5.5m Diam: 1m	Dry/Air Weight: 1,400kg Depth Rating: 3,000m Construction: Modular- Carbon fiber laminate material and syntactic foam IOC/Status: 1997

Energy, Endurance & Propulsion	Payload and Sensors
Energy System: 45kW.hr Al/HP semi fuel cell Energy Capacity: Range/Endurance: 60hrs @ 4 knots (with MBE, SSS, SBP, and CTD) Max Speed: 4 knots Propulsion:	Payload Capacity: Communication: Acoustic command, data links, RF, Iridium, Ethernet, WLAN Navigation: IMU, DVL, Depth, USBL, NavP TP Ranging, GPS, TerrNav Config/Actuators: Sonars/Sensors: Side Scan Sonar, Synthetic Aperture Sonar, Multibeam echo sounder, sub-bottom profiler

Figure 18.   UUV #15: HUGIN 3000

Country of Origin: Norway	**Hugin 4500**		Ref No: 16
	Provider: Kongsberg Gruppen		Source: www.km.kongsberg.com

Applications		**Features**
 L & R: Stinger based system	•Offshore surveying for oil and gas industry •Marine Research	Length: 6m Diam: 1m IOC/Status: 1997	Dry/Air Weight: 1,900kg Depth Rating: 4,500m Construction: Modular-Carbon fiber laminate material and syntactic foam

Energy, Endurance & Propulsion	**Payload and Sensors**
Energy System: 60 kW.hr Al/HP semi fuel cell Energy Capacity: Range/Endurance: 60hrs @ 4 knots (with MBE, SSS, SBP and CTD) Max Speed: 4 knots Propulsion:	Payload Capacity: Communication: Acoustic command, data links, RF, Iridium, Ethernet, WLAN Navigation: IMU, DVL, Depth, USBL, NavP TP Ranging, GPS, TerrNav Config/Actuators: Sonars/Sensors: Side Scan Sonar, Synthetic Aperture Sonar, Multibeam echo sounder, sub-bottom profiler

Figure 19.   UUV #16: HUGIN 4500

Country of Origin: Canada	**ISE ARCS**		Ref No: 17
	Provider: International Submarine Engineering Limited		Source: www.ise.bc.ca

Applications		**Features**
 L & R:	•AUV Research	Length: 21ft (6.4m) Diam: 27in (68.6cm)	Dry/Air Weight: 3,000 lbs (1,360.8kg) Depth Rating: 304.8m (1,000ft) Construction: IOC/Status: 1987

Energy, Endurance & Propulsion	**Payload and Sensors**
Energy System: 1 or 2 10kW.hr NiCd Energy Capacity: Range/Endurance: 22.5 or 45 miles (36 or 74 km) 10 hours with 300 lb payload with 20kW.hr Max Speed: 5.5 knots Propulsion: 2.5 HP brushless DC motor	Payload Capacity: 300 to 1,400 lbs Communication: Navigation: Honeywell MAPS 726 Inertial Navagation Unit Config/Actuators: Sonars/Sensors: EDO 3050 Doppler sonar, strain gage depth transducer

Figure 20.   UUV #17: ISE ARCS

Country of Origin:	ISE Explorer		Ref No: 18
Canada	Provider: International Submarine Engineering Limited		Source: www.ise.bc.ca

Applications	Features
•AUV Research	Dry/Air Weight: 750 to 1,250 kg
•Ocean Research	
	Length: 4.5 to 6.0m	Depth Rating: 300, 1,000, 3,000 or 5,000m
	Diam: .69 to .74m	Construction: Modular
L & R: Ship board winch	IOC/Status: 2001

Energy, Endurance & Propulsion	Payload and Sensors
	Payload Capacity: 200 kg
Energy System: 1.6kW.hr Lion	Communication: 900 or 2400 MHz radio, Iridium satellite communications
Energy Capacity:	
Range/Endurance: 120km on single battery bank	Navigation: IxSea Fiber-Optic or Kearfott Ring Laser Gyro INU, 300 or 600 kHz DVL, Kongsberg Digital Altimeter Control
Max Speed: 2.5 meters per second	Config/Actuators:
Propulsion:	Sonars/Sensors: Motorola GS antenna, USBL, depth sensor, Kearfott Ring Laser Gyro

Figure 21.   UUV #18: ISE Explorer

Country of Origin:	ISE Theseus		Ref No: 19
Canada	Provider: International Submarine Engineering Limited		Source: www.ise.bc.ca

Applications	Features
	Dry/Air Weight: 8,600kg
• Cable Laying	Depth Rating: 2,000m
	Length: 10.7m	Construction: Aluminum Pressure Hull
	Diam: 127cm	
L & R:	IOC/Status: 1992

Energy, Endurance & Propulsion	Payload and Sensors
	Payload Capacity: 550Kg (1,200lbs Dry) or 1,910kg (4,200lbs) Wet
Energy System: Up to 600kW.hr Lion	Communication:
Energy Capacity:	Navigation: 330kHz doppler sonar, terminal low frequency homing, IxSea INU, obstacle avoidance control
Range/Endurance: >1,360 km	
Max Speed: 2.5 meters per second	
Propulsion: 6 hp brushless dc motor and gearbox driving single propeller	Config/Actuators:
	Sonars/Sensors:

Figure 22.   UUV #19: ISE Theseus

Country of Origin: USA	IVER 2 580-EP (Expandable Payload)	Ref No: 20

Provider: OceanServer Technology, Inc   Source: www.iver-auv.com

Applications	Features
•Environmental Survey	Dry/Air Weight: 44 lbs (configuration dependent)
•Imaging Surveys	Depth Rating: 100m
•Bathymetry	
	Length: 30, 35 or 42 inches
	Construction:
L & R: Single Person L & R	Diam: 5.8 inches
	IOC/Status:

Energy, Endurance & Propulsion	Payload and Sensors
Energy System: 600-800WHrs Lion	Payload Capacity:
Energy Capacity:	Communication: Wireless 802.11g Ethernet
Range/Endurance: 8-14 hrs at 2.5 knots, configuration dependent	Navigation: GPS (WAAS corrected), depth sensors
Max Speed: 4 knots	Config/Actuators:
Propulsion: 3 blade propeller	Sonars/Sensors: many optional

Figure 23.   UUV #20: IVER 2 580-EP

Country of Origin: USA	IVER 2 580- S	Ref No: 21

Provider: OceanServer Technology, Inc   Source: www.iver-auv.com

Applications	Features
•Environmental Survey	Dry/Air Weight: 44lbs (standard vehicle)
•Imaging Surveys	Depth Rating: 100m
•Bathymetry	
	Length: 49.8 inches (without sensors)
	Construction:
L & R: Single Person L & R	Diam: 5.8 inches
	IOC/Status:

Energy, Endurance & Propulsion	Payload and Sensors
Energy System: 600-800Whrs Lion	Payload Capacity:
Energy Capacity:	Communication: 802.11g Ethernet
Range/Endurance: 8-14 hrs at 2.5 knots, configuration dependent	Navigation: GPS (WAAS corrected), depth sensors
Max Speed: 4 knots	Config/Actuators:
Propulsion: 3 blade propeller	Sonars/Sensors: many optional

Figure 24.   UUV #21: IVER 2 580-S

Country of Origin: USA	**As yet Unnamed**	Ref No: 22
	Provider: Advanced Solutions for Tomorrow	Source: www.asft.net

Applications	Features
•Underwater Surveys	Dry/Air Weight: 670-800 lbs
•Water Quality Assessment	Length:
•Port Protection	Diam:
	Depth Rating:
	Construction:
	IOC/Status:

Energy, Endurance & Propulsion	Payload and Sensors
Energy System: 2.5kW.hr – 8.4kW.hr depending on battery configuration	Payload Capacity:
Energy Capacity:	Communication: WiFi
Range/Endurance:	Navigation: DGPS<
Max Speed: 7 knots	Config/Actuators:
Propulsion:	Sonars/Sensors: many optional

Figure 25.   UUV #22: ASFT TBD

Country of Origin: USA	**Lockheed Martin Marlin MK1**	Ref No: 23
	Provider: Lockheed Martin Corp	Source: www.lockheedmartin.com

Applications	Features
•Inspection (pipeline, oil platform, ports, piers)	Dry/Air Weight: 1,000lbs (454kg)
•Sensor placement/retrieval	Depth Rating: 1,000ft (304m)
•Ocean/Wreckage surveying	Length: 5ft (1.5m)
	Width: 2.5ft (0.8m) Construction: Modular
	Height: 2.5ft (0.8m) IOC/Status:

Energy, Endurance & Propulsion	Payload and Sensors
Energy System:	Payload Capacity: 50-150 lbs (23 to 68kg)
Energy Capacity:	Communication: Acoustic modem, Ethernet, Irridium, WiFi, RF
Range/Endurance: 4 to 16 hours	Navigation: Doppler Aided Inertial Navigation, USBL
Max Speed: 8 knots	Config/Actuators:
Propulsion:	Sonars/Sensors: FLS, SLS, SAS, CTD, Bathymetric Sonar, ADCP, Sub bottom profiler, Turbidity, 3D Imaging Sonar
L & R: from ship	

Figure 26.   UUV #23: Lockheed Martin Marline MK1

Country of Origin:	**Lockheed Martin Marlin MK2**		Ref No: 24
USA	Provider: Lockheed Martin Corp	Source: www.lockheedmartin.com	

	Applications		**Features**
	•Inspection (pipeline, oil platform, ports, piers)		Dry/Air Weight: 2,100lbs (954kg)
			Depth Rating: 1,000-13,000ft (304-4,000m)
		Length: 10ft (3m)	
	•Sensor placement/retrieval	Width: 5ft (1.5m)	Construction: Modular
•Ocean/Wreckage surveying		Height: 4ft (1.3m)	IOC/Status:

Energy, Endurance & Propulsion	**Payload and Sensors**
	Payload Capacity: 250lbs (113kg)
Energy System:	Communication: Acoustic modem, Ethernet, Irridium, WiFi, RF
Energy Capacity:	
Range/Endurance: 18 to 24 hours	Navigation: Doppler Aided Inertial Navigation, GPS
Max Speed: 6 knots	
Propulsion:	Config/Actuators:
L & R: from ship	Sonars/Sensors: FLS, SLS, SAS, CTD, Bathymetric Sonar, ADCP, Sub bottom profiler, Turbidity, 3D Imaging Sonar

Figure 27.   UUV #24: Lockheed Martin Marline MK2

Country of Origin:	**Lockheed Martin Marlin MK3**		Ref No: 25
USA	Provider: Lockheed Martin Corp	Source: www.lockheedmartin.com	

	Applications		**Features**
	•Inspection (pipeline, oil platform, ports, piers)		Dry/Air Weight: 3,500lbs (1,590kg)
			Depth Rating: 1,000-13,000ft (304-4,000m)
		Length: 16ft (4.9m)	
	•Sensor placement/retrieval	Width: 5ft (1.5m)	Construction: Modular
•Ocean/Wreckage surveying		Height: 4ft (1.3m)	IOC/Status:

Energy, Endurance & Propulsion	**Payload and Sensors**
Energy System:	Payload Capacity: 250lbs (113kg)
Energy Capacity:	Communication: Acoustic modem, Ethernet, Irridium, WiFi, RF
Range/Endurance: 18 to 80 hours	
Max Speed: 6 knots	Navigation: Doppler Aided Inertial Navigation, GPS
Propulsion:	Config/Actuators:
L & R: from ship	Sonars/Sensors: FLS, SLS, SAS, CTD, Bathymetric Sonar, ADCP, Sub bottom profiler, Turbidity, 3D Imaging Sonar

Figure 28.   UUV #25: Lockheed Martin Marline MK3

Country of Origin: USA	REMUS 100		Ref No: 26
	Provider: Hydroid LLC	Source: www.hydroid.com	
Applications •Environmental Monitoring •Fishery Ops •Scientific Sampling •Mine Counter Measures (MCM) •Hydrographic Surveys •Harbor Security •Debris Field Mapping		Length: From 63in (160cm) Diam: 7.5in (19cm)	**Features** Dry/Air Weight: From <80lbs (37kg) Depth Rating: 100m Construction: Modular IOC/Status: 2001

Energy, Endurance & Propulsion	**Payload and Sensors**
Energy System: 1kW.hr Lion rechargeable Energy Capacity: Range/Endurance: 22 hours at optimum speed of 3 knots >8 hours at 5 knots, dependant on speed and sensor configuration Max Speed: Propulsion: Direct dive DC brushless motor to open 3-bladed propeller	Payload Capacity: Communication: Acoustic Communication, Iridium, WiFi, Gateway buoy Navigation: GPS, Digital Ultra Short Baseline (DUSBL), INS Config/Actuators: Sonars/Sensors: Acoustic Doppler, Current Profiling, LBL, Side Scan Sonar, Bathymetry L & R: Two Person Portable

Figure 29.   UUV #26: REMUS 100

Country of Origin: USA	REMUS 600		Ref No: 27
	Provider: Hydroid LLC	Source: www.hydroid.com	
Applications •Environmental Monitoring •Fishery Ops •Scientific Sampling •Mine Counter Measures (MCM) •Hydrographic Surveys •Harbor Security •Debris Field Mapping		Length: 128in (3.25m) depending on config. Diam: 12.75in (32.4cm)	**Features** Dry/Air Weight: 530lbs (240kg) Depth Rating: 600, 1,500, or 3,000m Construction: Modular IOC/Status: 2001

Energy, Endurance & Propulsion	**Payload and Sensors**
Energy System: 5.2kW.hr Lion rechargeable Energy Capacity: Range/Endurance: As long as 70 hours Max Speed: 5 knots Propulsion: Direct dive DC brushless motor to open 2-bladed propeller L & R: Launch and Recovery System	Payload Capacity: Communication: Acoustic Communications, Iridium, WiFi 2.4GHz, 100 base-T Ehternet Navigation: Inertial navigator, Long Baseline (LBL), acoustic, WAAS GPS, Ultra Short Baseline (USBL) Config/Actuators: Sonars/Sensors: Acoustic Doppler Current Profiling, Side Scan Sonar, Pressure, Conductivity & Temperature, Iridium, GPS

Figure 30.   UUV #27: REMUS 600

23

Country of Origin: USA	REMUS 6000		Ref No: 28
	Provider: Hydroid LLC	Source: www.hydroid.com	

	Applications		**Features**
•Environmental Monitoring	•Mine Counter Measures (MCM)		Dry/Air Weight: 1,900lbs (862kg)
	•Hydrographic Surveys		Depth Rating: 6,000m (4,000m also available)
•Fishery Ops	•Harbor Security		Length: 12.6ft (3.84m) Construction: Modular
•Scientific Sampling	•Debris Field Mapping		Diam: 28in (71cm) IOC/Status: 2001

Energy, Endurance & Propulsion	**Payload and Sensors**
Energy System: 11kW.hr Lion rechargeable	Payload Capacity:
Energy Capacity:	Communication: Acoustic modem, Iridium, 802.11B WiFi
Range/Endurance: 22 hours typical, subject to speed and sensor config	Navigation: Long Baseline Transducer, Dead Reckon with ADCP Inertial Navigation Unit
Max Speed: 5 knots	Config/Actuators:
Propulsion: Direct dive DC brushless motor to open 2-bladed propeller	Sonars/Sensors: Acoustic Doppler Current Profiling, INS, Side Scan Sonar, Pressure, Conductivity & Temperature, Iridium, GPS
L & R: Launch and Recovery System	

Figure 31. UUV #28: REMUS 6000

Country of Origin: Sweden	SAAB Double Eagle		Ref No: 29
	Provider: Saab Underwater Systems AB	Source: www.seaeye.com	

	Applications		**Features**
	•Mine Counter Measures (MCM)		Dry/Air Weight: 540kg
			Depth Rating: 500m (1,500 & 3,000m optional)
	•Mine Disposal	Length: 2.9m	Construction: Modular
		Width: 1.3m	IOC/Status:
L & R: Launch & Recovery System (LARS)		Height: 1.0m	

Energy, Endurance & Propulsion	**Payload and Sensors**
	Payload Capacity:
Energy System:	Communication: Gigabit Ethernet, WiFi, Radio Acoustic
Energy Capacity:	
Range/Endurance: 10+ hours (AUV mode)	Navigation: INS, DVL, GPS,
Max Speed: 8 knots	Config/Actuators:
Propulsion: Two 5KW brushless motors	Sonars/Sensors: Depth Sensor, leakage sensors, speed log

Figure 32. UUV #29: SAAB Double Eagle

Country of Origin: Sweden	SAAB AUV 62		Ref No: 30
	Provider: Saab Underwater Systems AB	Source: www.seaeye.com	

Applications	Features
•Mine Counter Measures (MCM) •ISR	Dry/Air Weight: 700-1,500kg config dependent
Length: 3m	Depth Rating: 200-500m
Width: 0.53m	Construction:
L & R: Crane, Stern Ramp, Submarine Tube Height: 0.53m	IOC/Status:

Energy, Endurance & Propulsion	Payload and Sensors
Energy System:	Payload Capacity:
Energy Capacity:	Communication:
Range/Endurance:	Navigation:
Max Speed: 5.14 meters per second	Config/Actuators:
Propulsion:	Sonars/Sensors:

Figure 33.　　　UUV #30: SAAB AUV 62

Country of Origin: USA	Seahorse I		Ref No: 31
	Provider: Penn State Univ Applied Research Lab	Source: www.arl.psu.edu	

Applications	Features
•Seabed Mapping	Dry/Air Weight: 10,000 lbs (4,490kg)
Length: 28 ft 6 in (8.66m)	Depth Rating: 1,000m
	Construction: IOC/Status:
L & R: Crane, Stern Ramp Diam: 38 inches	

Energy, Endurance & Propulsion	Payload and Sensors
Energy System: Alkaline	Payload Capacity: 10 cubic feet (approx.)
Energy Capacity: 166.183kWh	Communication: RF, Iridium, Limited Acoustic
Range/Endurance: 72 to 125 hours load dependent	Navigation: INS, GPS
Max Speed: 4.12 meters per second	Config/Actuators:
Propulsion: 5hp electric motor connected to 3 rotor blades	Sonars/Sensors: Side Scan, CTD, Acoustic Doppler Current Profiler

Figure 34.　　　UUV #31: ARL/PSU Seahorse I

Country of Origin:	Seahorse II		Ref No: 32
USA	Provider: Penn State Univ Applied Research Lab		Source: www.arl.psu.edu

Applications	Features
•Seabed Mapping	Dry/Air Weight: 10,000 lbs (4,490kg)
	Depth Rating: 1,000m
Length: 28 ft 6 in (8.66m)	Construction: IOC/Status:
L & R: Crane, Stern Ramp	Diam: 38 inches	

Energy, Endurance & Propulsion	Payload and Sensors
Energy System: Alkaline	Payload Capacity: 10 cubic feet (approx.)
Energy Capacity: 166.183KWh	Communication: RF, Iridium, Limited Acoustic
Range/Endurance: 72 to 125 hours load dependent	Navigation: INS, GPS
	Config/Actuators:
Max Speed: 5.14 meters per second	Sonars/Sensors: Side Scan, CTD, Acoustic Doppler Current Profiler
Propulsion: 5hp electric motor connected to 3 rotor blades	

Figure 35.   UUV #32: ARL/PSU Seahorse II

Country of Origin:	Ranger		Ref No: 33
USA	Provider: iRobot Corporation		Source: www.irobot.com

	Applications		Features
	•Environmental Monitoring		Dry/Air Weight: 9.07kg
	•Freshwater Mapping		Depth Rating:
	•Marine Sciences Survey	Length: 0.86m	Construction:
•Sensor Development	•Oceanographic Survey	Width: 0.09m	IOC/Status:
•REA	•Vehicle Research	Height: 0.09m	

Energy, Endurance & Propulsion	Payload and Sensors
	Payload Capacity:
Energy System:	Communication:
Energy Capacity:	Navigation:
Range/Endurance:	Config/Actuators:
Max Speed:	Sonars/Sensors:
Propulsion:	
L & R: Hand Held, Single Person Portable	

Figure 36.   UUV #33: iRobot Ranger

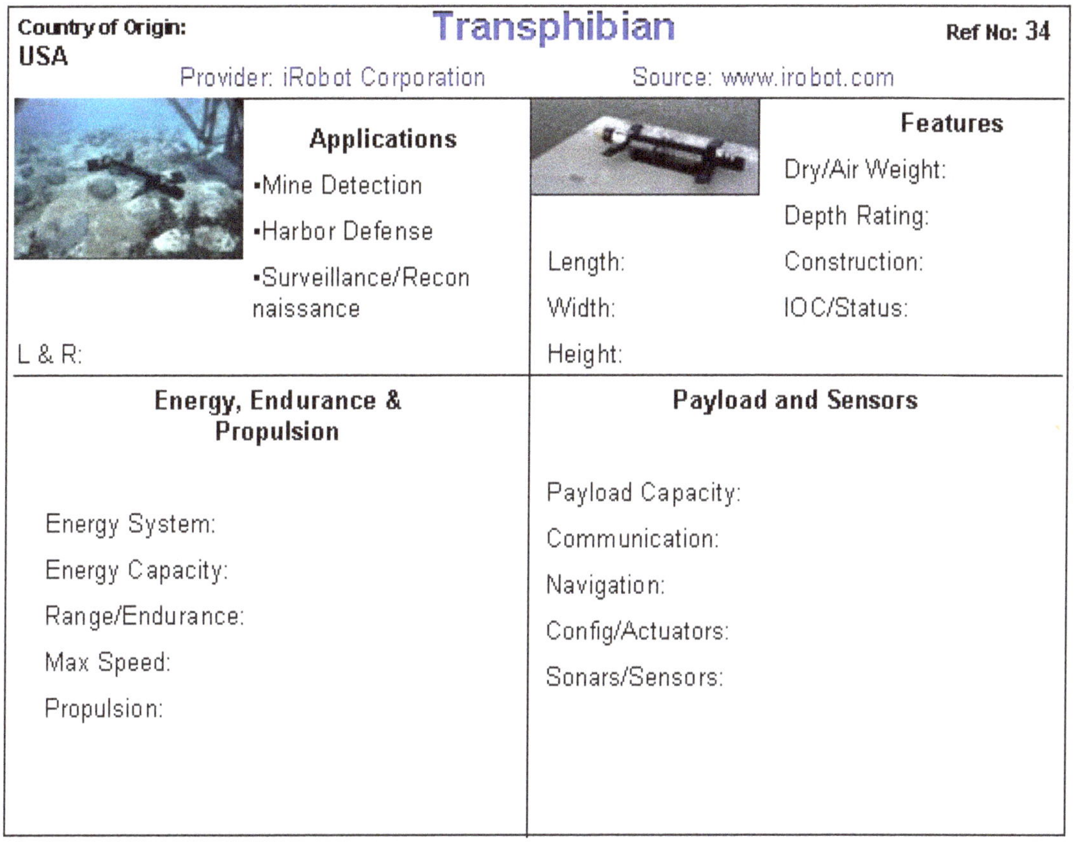

Country of Origin: USA	Transphibian		Ref No: 34
Provider: iRobot Corporation		Source: www.irobot.com	

	Applications		**Features**
	• Mine Detection		Dry/Air Weight:
	• Harbor Defense		Depth Rating:
	• Surveillance/Recon naissance	Length:	Construction:
		Width:	IOC/Status:
L & R:		Height:	

Energy, Endurance & Propulsion	**Payload and Sensors**
Energy System:	Payload Capacity:
Energy Capacity:	Communication:
Range/Endurance:	Navigation:
Max Speed:	Config/Actuators:
Propulsion:	Sonars/Sensors:

Figure 37.   UUV #34: iRobot Ranger

C.   CHAPTER SUMMARY

This chapter presents the results of a web-based commercial UUV survey. The thirty four UUV systems investigated form the selection set that this study chooses from for further system architectural analysis and discussion. The UUV systems surveyed are presented in a quad-chart format that listed available information in applications, features, energy/endurance/propulsion and payload/sensors. There are fifteen different UUV providers offering the thirty four systems. The surveyed systems were intentionally targeted from the commercial sector; low (or no) production academic and laboratory based UUV's and military systems are also not considered for this survey.

THIS PAGE INTENTIONALLY LEFT BLANK

III. SELECTION OF UUV SYSTEMS, SIGNIFICANT UUV ARCHITECTURAL ATTRIBUTES AND SYSTEM CONSIDERATIONS THAT INFLUENCE THESE ATTRIBUTES

A. INTRODUCTION

This chapter presents what are considered prevalent or "high production" commercial UUV systems that were selected as a basis for this system architecture analysis and discussion. There are five of these high-production commercial UUV systems. In addition, three other UUV systems are discussed, which are *not* found to be produced in significant quantity, but are found to have established (i.e., experience) presence in at-sea operations. These "low-production" UUV systems have interesting features and uniquely support the architecture discussion. This chapter also discusses comprehensively the significant UUV architectural attributes selected for study. System level considerations that influence these architectural attributes are also presented.

B. UUV SYSTEM SELECTIONS

For this study, five UUV systems were considered prevalent and "highly-produced" and substantially embedded in the UUV commercial marketplace. It is important to note that other UUV systems produced by these providers are also be discussed from an architecture perspective. For example, the REMUS family of vehicles (100, 600 and 6000) are *all* be analyzed when particular architectural attributes are discussed. Another example is the Gavia AUV system consists of three different AUV systems that are discussed during this study. The five high-production UUV systems selected for this system architecture analysis and discussion are:

- Hyroid REMUS 600 et al.
- Kongsberg HUGIN 1000,... et al.
- ISE Explorer
- Bluefin-12 AUV,... et al.
- Hafmynd Gavia AUV System

These particular UUV systems were selected based on three considerations. The primary selection criteria used was "market presence," meaning the UUV systems had a significant presence in the marketplace in terms of multiple applications, diverse customers and "several" delivered UUV systems to users/customers. After conducting the UUV market survey and researching articles and journals, it was apparent that few UUV providers have documented "multiple" sales. A substantial amount of sales was an indicator of a more mature product for this analysis. The second consideration component was indication that the UUV providers delivered their UUV systems complete for operational use and "stepped away" to let users operate independently from the provider. This criterion was met by these five UUV providers by showing (in researched advertisements, papers and articles) mission control, launch and recovery, tracking and other *field* equipment. Other UUV systems investigated, from academia, for example, do not advertise convincing amounts of existing field equipment that indicates "full system" delivery and encouragement that the buyer can operate the UUV system independently of the provider. The third selection metric used, which has already been alluded to, was the availability of suitable open-source information for this study. Numerous references have been obtained for each UUV system in order to acquire suitable material for meaningful architectural discussion and analysis. The fact that REMUS, Hydroid, ISE, Bluefin and Hafmynd offer a variety of UUV system configurations permits more interesting discussion of system construct, features and associated drivers.

Three other UUV systems are analyzed during this study, but are *not* considered highly produced and as established (i.e., quantity) in the marketplace. However, these three low-production systems have significant experience at-sea and offer unique architectural attributes that support this analysis/discussion. The three low-production UUV systems selected for system architecture analysis and discussion are:

- Boeing Echo Ranger
- Lockheed Martin Marlin
- Naval Oceanographic Office Seahorse

These low-production UUV systems also meet the third UUV system selection criteria mentioned above: suitable open-source information for this study.

1.   Hydroid REMUS (USA)

Hydroid's Remote Environmental Monitoring Units (REMUS) family of UUV systems is designated by its name and operational depth (number). For example, a REMUS 600 is a REMUS system designed to operate with an operational depth limit of 600 meters (1969 ft). Hydroid currently offers [4] REMUS 100, REMUS 600, REMUS 1500, REMUS 3000 and REMUS 6000 UUV systems. Hydroid UUV systems are well established in the marketplace with a substantial amount of system deliveries. According to a RAND UUV Study [5], Hydroid had built 174 REMUS systems by the end of 2007. Figure 38 shows a picture of a REMUS 100. Figure 39 shows a picture of a REMUS 600 and Figure 40 shows a picture of a REMUS 6000.

Figure 38.   REMUS 100, from [4].

Figure 39.   REMUS 600, from [6].

Figure 40.   REMUS 6000, from [7].

2.   Kongsberg HUGIN (Norway)

Similar to REMUS, the Kongsberg HUGIN UUV system naming convention is also designated by operational depth in meters, i.e., HUGIN 1000. Kongsberg currently offers [8] HUGIN 1000, HUGIN 3000 and HUGIN 4500. According to [9] and [10], HUGIN UUV systems began in-water operations in 1992 and by 2005 there were eight HUGINs sold to military and commercial customers and two more built for demonstrations. Figure 41 shows a picture of a Kongsberg HUGIN 1000 and Figure 42 shows a picture of a Kongsberg HUGIN 4500.

Figure 41.   Konsgberg's HUGIN 1000, from [9].

Figure 42.   Konsgberg's HUGIN 4500, from [9].

3. ISE Explorer (Canada)

The International Submarine Engineering (ISE) Explorer was based on corporate knowledge of two ISE UUV predecessors: Theseus and ARCS. ISE currently offers [11] four depth-rated versions of Explorer; 300, 1000, 3000 and 5000 meter versions. According to [12] and [13], ISE has a broad array of customers and as of November 2008, had delivered seven Explorer UUV systems. Figure 43 shows a photo of ISE's Explorer.

Figure 43.   ISE's Explorer, from [14].

4. Bluefin AUV (USA)

Bluefin Robotics Autonomous Undersea Vehicles (AUV) come with cylindrical body diameters in their name designators, for example, Bluefin-12 is a 12-inch (cylindrical) diameter UUV. Bluefin currently offers [15] Bluefin-9, Bluefin-12 and Bluefin-21. Bluefin also advertises a 21 inch variant called Bluefin-BPAUV (Battlespace Preparation AUV), gliders, and a line of submersible (UUV's) lithium-ion batteries.

According to [16], Bluefin Robotics has produced fifty AUV platforms as of the end of 2006. Figure 44 shows Bluefin-9, Figure 45 shows Bluefin-12 and Figure 46 shows Bluefin-BPAUV.

Figure 44.   Bluefin-BPAUV (21 inch (cylindrical) diameter), from [15].

Figure 45.   Bluefin-12, from [15].

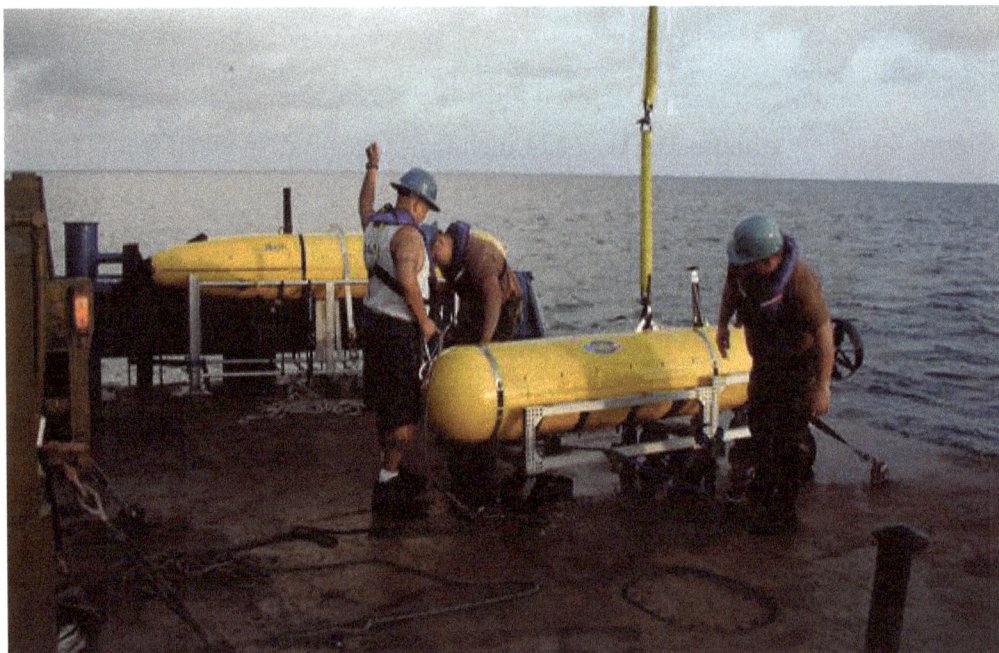

Figure 46.   Bluefin-BPAUV (21 inch (cylindrical) diameter), from [15].

5. Hafmynd Gavia (Iceland)

Hafmynd Ehf's Gavia, meaning "great northern diver" [17], AUV family consists of three versions configured for specific missions: the Offshore, Scientific and Defence according to [18]. They also have depth designators attached to the Gavia name. For example, Gavia 200 is rated for operational depths of 200m. The Gavia AUVs are another relatively small UUV system with a cylindrical body diameter of 0.2 meters (7.87 inches) with operational depth options of 200, 500, 1000 and 2000 meters [19]. As of 2010, there were over 20 Gavia AUV systems delivered according to [17]. Figure 47 shows the three Gavia AUV versions available from Hafmynd. Figure 48 shows a Gavia Offshore in the field.

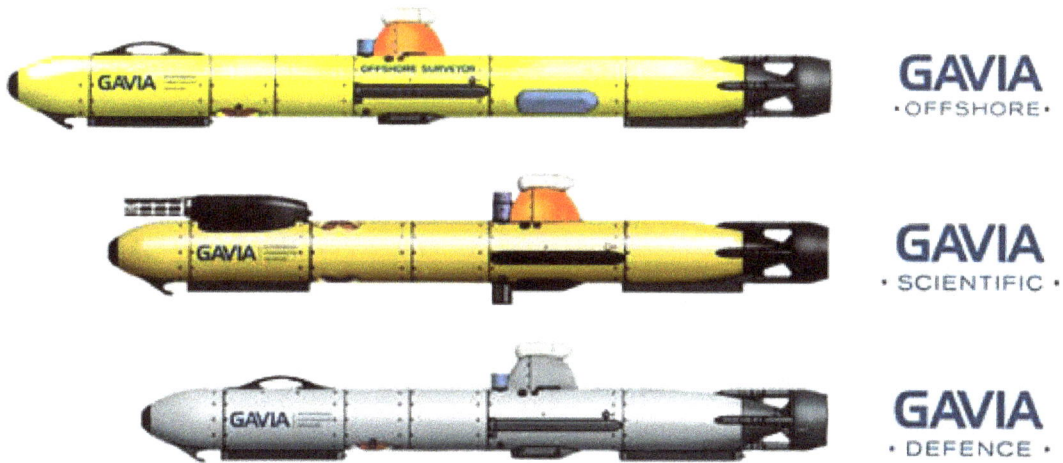

Figure 47.   Hafmynd's Gavia AUV Family, from [18].

Figure 48.   Gavia Offshore at Caspian Sea, from [18].

6.   Boeing Echo Ranger (USA)

Boeing's Echo Ranger is one of the "low-production" UUV systems selected for this study. According to [20], the Echo Ranger is a large UUV developed for the commercial oil survey industry. The Echo Ranger has been operational since 2004 [1]. This large displacement UUV (LDUUV) is 50 inch x 50 inch x 18 feet long, weighs ~11,700 lbs (in air), carries ~977 lbs of payload and has an operation depth of 10,000 feet (3048 meters). Figure 49 shows the Boeing Echo Ranger.

Figure 49.   Boeing's Echo Ranger, from [1].

7.   Lockheed Martin Marlin

Lockheed Martin's Marlin is relatively new to the market and was introduced during the OCEANS '09 conference [21]. This is another "low-production" UUV system, which is available [22] in three variants: Mk1, Mk2 and Mk2. Each Marlin variant has different operational depth ratings (305m, 1000m and 4000m) and increasingly large payload volumes. The Marlin targets inspection and maintenance missions, with a focus on the oil industry, and is based on 50+ years of maritime undersea systems experience [23]. Figure 50 shows Lockheed Martin's Marlin.

Figure 50.   Lockheed Martin's Marlin, from [24].

8.   Naval Oceanographic Office (NAVOCEANO) Seahorse

NAVOCEANO's Seahorse initial construction began in April 1999, and was delivered for testing in May 2000, three Seahorse systems have been provided to NAVOEANO. According to [25], the developer was the Applied Research Laboratory, Penn State University. This is the final low-production UUV system being introduced in this discussion. The Seahorse is a 38-inch diameter, 28-foot long, and 11,300-pound displacement vehicle. The system was designed to be deployed from T-AGS PATHFINDER class research ships [25]. The maximum operational depth of the Seahorse is 1000m [1]. Figure 51 shows NAVOCEANO's Seahorse.

Figure 51.   Naval Oceanographic Office's Seahorse Developed by Applied Research
Laboratory, Penn State University, from [26].

C.   SIGNIFICANT ARCHITECTURAL ATTRIBUTES AND SYSTEM CONSIDERATIONS THAT INFLUENCE THEM

With UUV systems selected for architecture related analysis and discussion, the architectural features of choice for the UUV systems need to be defined. This thesis is intended to provide an overview of UUV systems and associated architectural attributes of interest; the following seven groups of attributes are investigated:

- Overall Vehicle Arrangement (Layout)
- Form Factor, Propulsors & Control Surfaces
- Energy System
- Pressure Hulls and Wet Volume
- Accommodations for Sensors
- Communications
- Launch & Recovery

41

1. Overall Vehicle Arrangement

The vehicle arrangement or layout is a result of UUV form factor, the (geometric) inventory of UUV components and interface requirements for various equipment and/or sensors. The arrangements of these UUV systems are analyzed to introduce vehicle configurations and features, including: vehicle form factor, control surfaces and movers (propulsors), energy components, pressure hull and flooded regions, sensors, communications equipment and launch and recovery hardware. These layouts also allow a reference and basis for further discussion as the analysis progresses. Vehicle layouts are presented and discussed in Chapter IV.

2. Form Factor, Propulsors and Control Surfaces

The UUV's form factor is typically inspired by desire for smooth hydrodynamic form (i.e., low drag), since power on any battery powered system is usually at a premium and certain (higher) speeds may not be obtainable or efficient with higher drag shapes. The UUVs being studied have similar "torpedo" shapes with different length-to-diameter ratios and cross-sectional geometries. Other drivers for form factors are launch and recovery methods, specific optimal speeds and vehicle flow noise requirements.

Propulsor (i.e., propellers and shrouded pump-jets) configurations on UUV systems vary, but have been found to generally fall into three design types:

1. Single rotating propeller (open or shrouded). A single propeller will generate torque, or twisting force on the UUV, which will need to be overcome or "countered" by the vehicle's control surfaces, static ballasting, or both.

2. Twin counter-rotating propellers (open or shrouded). The counter rotating propellers exert torque in opposite directions to help balance the rotational force on the vehicle. This reduces effort and demand from the vehicles control surfaces to maintain steady flight.

3. Single propeller-like rotor shrouded with pre-swirl stators. In this configuration, the pre-swirl stators (which are upstream of the rotating propulsor) induce a more efficient flow into the rotor and also create a counter-torque in the process.

The control surfaces of the UUV provide dynamic control of the vehicle and are sized to maintain vehicle fin authority at slow speed. One UUV system presented, the Bluefin-21, utilizes a gimbaled propulsor that vectors flow for UUV control and steerage in lieu of active control surfaces. Control surfaces are configured differently for the UUV systems presented. This is illustrated later in this study. Control surfaces typically reside aft on the UUV close to the propulsor. Some UUV's (e.g., ISE Explorer) also have implemented canards into their architecture, which are active control surfaces more forward on the UUV body.

3.   Energy System

The UUV's energy source, typically a battery or fuel cell, is a major component of the UUV's architecture, which drives system performance, mainly in terms of on-board power, system endurance and vehicle speed. It should be noted that primary batteries are not rechargeable (i.e., typical flashlight alkaline) and secondary batteries are re-chargeable (i.e., nickel-cadmium, lithium-ion for cordless power tools).

Several battery chemistries are available for UUV system use and selection of an energy choice is an important factor in the system design. Figure 52, from [27], shows common secondary battery technologies in terms of energy per unit weight or Watt-hours per kilogram (Wh/kg) and energy per unit size or Watt-hours per Liter (Wh/L). This figure clearly shows the family of lithium-ion cells provides much smaller size and much lower weight for a given stored energy when compared with the other most common battery technologies [27]. In particular, [27] shows size and weight are reduced up to four times if compared with the most common battery type, the lead-acid battery.

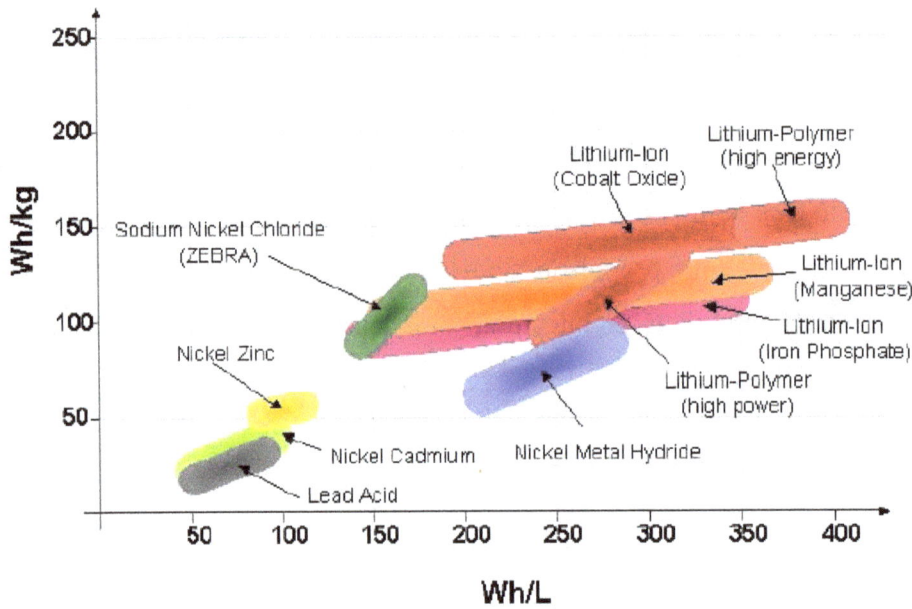

Figure 52.   Energy storage performance of different technologies, from [27].

It is not a surprise that most UUV systems investigated in this study utilize lithium-ion secondary batteries in their system architecture due to their high specific power and energy densities. Another tool for UUV energy source comparisons is a Ragone plot, which shows available energy with the relationship between specific energy and specific power. Figure 53, from [28], shows a typical Ragone energy availability plot. The vertical axis represents specific energy, in Wh/Kg, and the horizontal axis represents specific power in Watts per Kilogram (W/Kg). Specific energy is indicative of a vehicles range or endurance and specific power is indicative of a vehicle's higher power needs, such as acceleration. The diagonal dashed lines on Figure 53 represent *time* at that particular energy-power level. Capacitors are shown as substantially high power storage; but, note the time that power is available is only in seconds. In the context of this study, this figure (also) shows lithium-ion superiority (over nickel metal hydride (Ni-MH) and lead-acid).

For comparative purposes, Figure 53 shows fuel cells and internal combustion (IC) engines as comparison points even though their energy storage should be treated separately [27]. The IC engine is significantly superior to the common battery

44

chemistries, but not a common solution for typical UUV applications due to the complexity of supplying air, storing or removing engine exhaust, and compensating for changes in vehicle buoyancy while conducting a mission. Finally, the other points on Figure 53 are electric vehicle (EV), hybrid electric vehicle (HEV) and plug-in hybrid electric vehicle (PHEV) which are design objectives in the automotive industry.

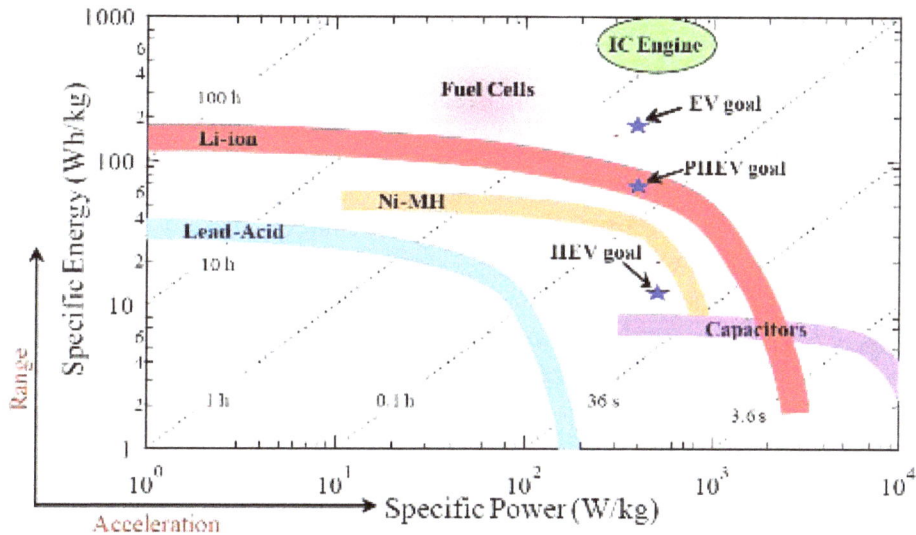

Figure 53.   Ragone plot for different energy storage solutions, from [28].

There are multiple energy-related considerations a system architect must consider when developing a UUV system. Linden, in [29], lists fifteen major design considerations for typical battery selection. This list is very comprehensive and very much represents what UUV system level considerations should be made. Linden's list of battery system selection considerations is shown in Figure 54.

45

1. *Type of Battery:* Primary, secondary, or reserve system
2. *Electrochemical System:* Matching of the advantages and disadvantages and of the battery characteristics with major equipment requirements
3. *Voltage:* Nominal or operating voltage, maximum and minimum permissible voltages, voltage regulation, profile of discharge curve, start-up time, voltage delay
4. *Load Current and Profile:* Constant current, constant resistance, or constant power; or others; value of load current or profile, single-valued or variable load, pulsed load
5. *Duty Cycle:* Continuous or intermittent, cycling schedule if intermittent
6. *Temperature Requirements:* Temperature range over which operation is required
7. *Service Life:* Length of time operation is required
8. *Physical Requirements:* Size, shape, weight; terminals
9. *Shelf Life:* Active/reserve battery system; state of charge during storage; storage time a function of temperature, humidity and other conditions
10. *Charge-Discharge Cycle (if Rechargeable):* Float or cycling service; life or cycle requirement; availability and characteristics of charging source; charging efficiency
11. *Environmental Conditions:* Vibration, shock, spin, acceleration, etc.; atmospheric conditions (pressure, humidity, etc.)
12. *Safety and Reliability:* Permissible variability, failure rates; freedom from outgassing or leakage; use of potentially hazardous or toxic components; type of effluent or signature gases or liquids, high temperature, etc.; operation under severe or potentially hazardous conditions; environmentally friendly
13. *Unusual or Stringent Operating Conditions:* Very long-term or extreme-temperature storage, standby, or operation; high reliability for special applications; rapid activation for reserve batteries, no voltage delay; special packaging for batteries (pressure vessels, etc.); unusual mechanical requirements, e.g., high shock or acceleration, nonmagnetic
14. *Maintenance and Resupply:* Ease of battery acquisition, accessible distribution; ease of battery replacement; available charging facilities; special transportation, recovery, or disposal procedures required
15. *Cost:* Initial cost; operating or life-cycle cost; use of critical or exotic (costly) materials

Figure 54.   Battery selection considerations, from [29].

Additionally, there are battery modules used in UUVs (i.e., Bluefin and HUGIN) that reside in the seawater flooded section, this drives special considerations to pressure tolerance, water tight integrity and special cabling/connection considerations. Another architecture consideration not explicitly defined in Linden's lists is accessibility for maintenance, removal and re-charging. Another consideration related to safety is monitoring requirements. For example, lithium-ion battery systems typically have individual cell voltage monitors and users may require cell temperature sensors as well.

4.   Pressure Hulls and Wet Volume

Another important system attribute for UUV architecture is the utilization of pressure hulls, free-flood volume, and (commonly) the combination of both. The UUV system architectures presented utilize dry pressure volumes typically housed in cylindrical or spherical structural vessels along with varying allocations for free-flood regions within the UUV form factor. The transition from free-flood to dry pressure hulls usually occurs with the utilization of a bulkhead with hull penetrations to accommodate waterproof connectors/cabling which is discussed later. Key architectural system considerations for pressure hulls in UUV design are:

a.   Operating Depth and Pressure Vessel Geometry

A substantial driver for UUV pressure hulls is depth pressure and the requirement for watertight (dry) volumes. Lesser depth requirements for the UUVs tends to result in cylindrical (larger percentage of vehicle volume) pressure vessels, Examples of this are the design of the REMUS 100 (100m) and the REMUS 600 (600m). The UUVs that have deeper depth capabilities tend to build spherical (smaller percentage of vehicle volume) pressure vessels. Examples of this are the design of the HUGIN 1000 (1000m) and the Boeing Echo Ranger (3000m). In contrast to a dominant "one or the other" pressure vessel tendency, one UUV system, the ISE Explorer (2200m), utilizes a cylindrical pressure vehicle with full hemi-spherical end bulkheads. The ISE design is closer to an even allocation of pressure vessel to flooded volume. This is investigated further.

b. Materials Used

The material used for the UUV pressure hulls varies with provider's preference and depth requirements. As shown in [1], AUVAC investigated hull materials used for several UUV system pressure vessels and found common materials utilized were:

- ABS (acrylonitrile butadiene styrene or thermoplastic)
- Acrylic
- Aluminum
- Carbon Fiber

- Fiberglass

- Graphite Epoxy

- GRP (glass reinforced plastic)

- HDPE (high density polyethylene)

- Steel

- Titanium

Figure 55 is AUVAC's, see [1], hull material "infographic," which shows the hull materials used on many different UUV systems. The figure does not specify which vehicle corresponds to each data point, but illustrates vehicle depth capability, vehicle size and the hull material choice. Note the diminishing use of steel and aluminum (less expensive materials) when depths increase beyond 2,000 meters. The "deeper divers" tend to utilize HDPE, GRP, ABS and titanium. Also note the many hull material N/A's (not available). As discussed later, the deeper diving UUVs with non-metallic materials tend to use spherical pressure vessels. Strength of the material is not the only consideration suggested in terms of pressure vessel material—corrosive properties, reactions (i.e., galvanic) with other materials and cost are substantial material considerations as well.

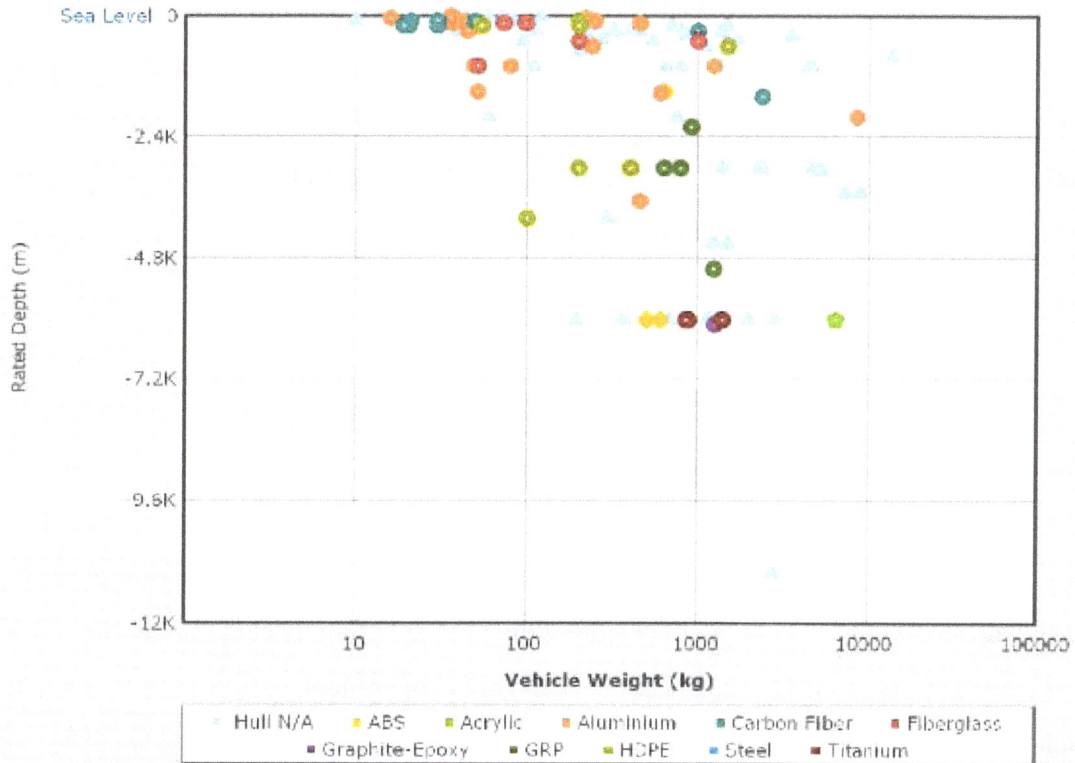

Figure 55.   AUVAC's hull material "infographic," from [1].

c. Buoyancy

Buoyancy of a UUV is a function of the vehicle's overall displacement, its weight and the density of the water it is operating in. UUV systems compensate for positive and negative buoyancy by utilizing different methods such as; 1. "driving through it" utilizing vehicle speed, vehicle pitch and forces from control surfaces, 2. pumping or flooding ballast tanks (with seawater) manipulating the vehicles buoyancy, and 3. utilizing thrusters as needed in the vertical plane of flight. The buoyancy of large UUVs that have substantial volumetric displacement will experience significant changes in buoyancy, even with small changes in water density. As a result, the larger UUV systems tend to have means of buoyancy manipulation.

Manipulated or variable buoyancy is a limited margin influencing the system displacement. However, and larger "static" measures are taken to compensate for UUV vehicle trim issues, and provide a more balanced weight-to-displacement relationship.

Common solutions to larger negative buoyancy issues are placement of syntactic foam (i.e., something less dense than seawater that will not crush at depth pressure) in free flood regions and increased empty volume (i.e., air voids) in the pressure vessels. A common solution to larger positive buoyancy issues is solid ballast (i.e., dense metals) in both dry and flooded vehicle regions.

d. Structural Challenges

Structural challenges for UUV architecture extends beyond consideration to structural integrity against hydro-static pressure. Considerations must be made for water pressure buckling effects (i.e., on long cylindrical pressure vessels), accommodations for penetrations and hull bosses (for cable connectors and sensors) which can cause high localized stress and volumetric considerations for efficient packaging in the UUV's configuration (layout). Other structural challenges for system design include handling, launch & recovery and specific mission requirements (i.e., anchoring).

e. Access and Maintenance

Maintainability and access to the UUV's components and sub-systems is another key consideration in pressure hull-related UUV architectural design. The UUV systems presented have varying accommodations for vehicle turn-around (i.e., battery recharge and data extraction) and system access for maintenance and repair.

5. Accommodations for Sensors

Sensing is a critical function for UUVs; system providers have implemented multitudes of sensors that are integrated into the overall vehicle architecture. Sensors for UUV systems include devices for measuring depth, altitude, water conductivity, water temperature, water density, geo-location and chemicals (to name a few). Other sensors, such as sonar, are used to obtain bottom imagery, objects in the water column, bathymetry, speed over the bottom and water-current profiling. The UUV systems presented offer a variety of such sensors and a discussion of their function and integration into the UUV occurs later. Key architectural system considerations for sensors in UUV design are:

a. Relative Location

The location of most sensors in UUV architecture is intentional even though there is an occasional last minute "strap-on" appearance. Most sensors have specific operational requirements including direct interface to sea-water, exposure to the external vehicle flow and directional (i.e., forward or downward looking) orientation. The UUV systems presented in this study were selected in part for purposes of discussion on sensor implementation.

b. Proximity to Emitters (Compatibility)

Some sensors are sensitive to other UUV stimulus such as electrical or mechanical noise, antenna radiation (i.e., electro-magnetic interference) and other vehicle self-noise sources.

c. Vulnerability

Many of the sensors presented have a requirement to be directly exposed to seawater (i.e., flush or exposed in the flow). Having exposed or even protruding sensors exposes vulnerability to impact, entanglement and other damage during handling, testing and operations.

d. Testability

Sensors may require access with the UUV full-up and ready for operations for pre-run system test or some other functional test of the sensor. The location of the sensors for testing may impact system design.

6.   Communications

Another key function discussed with sensors is communications equipment, i.e., antennas. It is understood that an argument could be made that the communication systems on UUVs could be in the "sensor" discussion. However, since all UUVs selected for discussion have communication gear, they are discussed individually. The communications devices on UUVs generally fall within two categories:

- Through Water Communications (i.e., acoustic communications or ACOMMS)
- Through Air Communications (i.e., Radio Frequency (RF) and Satellite Communications (SATCOM)

Key system architecture considerations for UUV communications are:

1. <u>Antenna height above water line</u>.

Antenna height is related to effective range of communications with a surfaced UUV, particularly with RF (line of sight) communications. The SATCOM antennas (i.e., commercial Iridium) have sensitivity to both wash-over and water surface backscatter, which is also effected by antenna height. There is an obvious trade for a system architect to consider between antenna height, vehicle system impacts, antenna motion (i.e., roll) and vehicle balance that needs to be considered when integrating an antenna system into a UUV.

2. <u>Communications Protocol and Data Handling</u>

There may be communication requirements (commercial or military) that drive what UUV data formats and communication standards are used. For example, the commercial Iridium (SATCOM) system utilizes its own data/message format via a transceiver in the UUV. RF communications could typically utilize Institute of Electrical and Electronics Engineers (IEEE) 802.11. UUV systems may elect to encrypt data as well. The data format, message handling and on-board UUV hardware to manage communication requirements should be considered in UUV architecture.

3. <u>Protection of External Hardware (i.e., antennas) from Sea Water and Pressure</u>

Selection of antennas and communication systems includes consideration to the available antennas and how they can be protected from the UUV's operational environment. There are also material considerations when trying to "protect" the UUV's antennas. A dome or housing in which an antenna is "encapsulated" may degraded (or even eliminate) the antenna's effectiveness.

4.   Location and Integration of Hardware

Acoustic communications (ACOMMS) transceivers (projectors and receivers) need to be integrated into the UUV with considerations to interface with seawater and the location on the UUV hull. ACOMMS transceivers are typically exposed directly to seawater, all UUV systems presented here have ACOMMS gear hull mounted and visible. Some UUV systems, i.e., Hydroid's REMUS 600, have the transceivers typically mounted on the lower portions of the UUV so underwater communications with surface support craft can occur when the vehicle is on the surface. Other UUV systems, i.e., HUGIN 1000, have the ACOMMS gear "higher" on UUV body to suit the deep diving UUV's through-water communications with surface support craft. These operational or CONOPS related requirements are significant communication considerations in the UUV's overall architecture.

7.   Launch and Recovery

The launch and recovery of the UUV systems presented utilize different ways to release and grapple (capture) the vehicle, but all share the common characteristic of surface ship deployment, operations base and recovery. The CONOPS of launch, operations and recovery impacts the development strategy of several UUV sub-systems including communications, structure, hull form, sensor locations, sensor selection, control functionality, related vehicle functionality and others. These UUV operational CONOPS are perhaps one of the most important considerations to a UUV's architecture.

Two approaches to vehicle capture are submerged vehicle capture with a homing and docking technique, and surfaced vehicle capture. The UUV systems discussed incorporate both of these methods, and are further discussed. More specifically, some submerged in-flight UUVs capture a vertical cable and are essentially reeled into a base or cage, other systems swim into a submerged cage and others are grappled on the surface and reeled onto the stern of the surface support craft.

D. CHAPTER SUMMARY

The purpose of this chapter is to present UUV systems selected for purposes of this study and discuss system architectural considerations that are analyzed more closely in the following chapter.

The vehicles selected represent systems that are mature in the marketplace with significant sales and market presence. The other UUV systems selected offer support for architectural discussion and analysis. An important factor in all system selections were the availability of sufficient open source information.

Significant architectural attributes and considerations that influence them were discussed. The major attributes selected were overall vehicle arrangement, form factor, propulsors and control surfaces, energy system, pressure hulls and wet volume, accommodations for sensors, communications, and launch and recovery.

IV. COMPARISON OF UUV ARCHITECTURAL ATTRIBUTES

A. INTRODUCTION

This chapter makes a comparison of UUV system attributes. The selected UUV systems (or family of systems) introduced in Chapter III, are the focus of this comparison. Other UUV systems may be introduced when their particular design characteristics support specific thesis discussion of architectural features, design attributes, Navy applications, etc. The following key attributes are investigated further:

1. Overall Vehicle Arrangement (Layout)
2. Form Factor, Propulsors & Control Surfaces
3. Energy System
4. Pressure Hulls and Wet Volume
5. Accommodations for Sensors
6. Communications
7. Launch & Recovery

Discussion follows, regarding how the UUV systems compare for each of these key attributes. Similarities, differences and trends are analyzed and discussed in the context of system architecture.

B. ANALYSIS OF UUV SYSTEM ATTRIBUTES

The selected UUV systems are analyzed central to each of the seven key attributes mentioned above. Information (that was both pertinent and available) is presented for an understanding of the "end state" of each of the UUV systems regarding these architectural attributes.

The five high-production UUV systems selected for this system architecture attribute analysis and discussion are:

1. REMUS 600, et al.
2. Kongsberg HUGIN 1000
3. ISE Explorer

4. Bluefin-12 AUV

5. Hafmynd Gavia AUV System

The three low production UUV systems selected to support key discussion points of system architecture analysis and discussion are:

1. Boeing Echo Ranger

2. Lockheed Martin Marlin

2. NAVOCEANO Seahorse

1.   REMUS 600

a.   REMUS Layout

The REMUS 600 external layout is shown in Figure 56. An internal component layout of this system could not be found. The layout illustrates vehicle sections and equipment/sensors that are "exposed" to the external flow around the vehicle form factor including; an open single propeller, aft control surfaces (fins), battery recharging port, airborne communications antenna, transducers for current profiling, navigation and acoustic communications, sonar transducers for imagery, forward control surfaces (fins) and recovery gear.

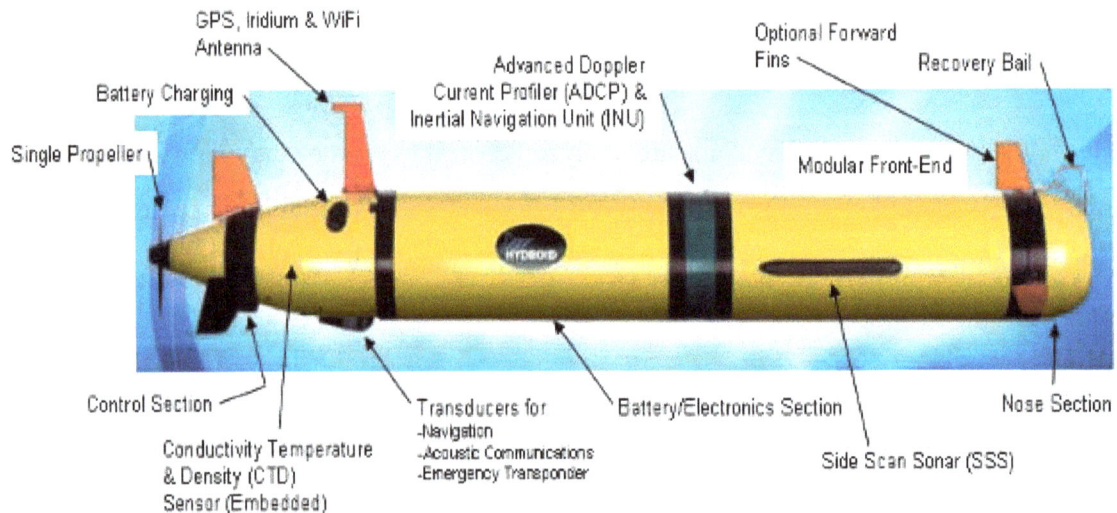

Figure 56.   REMUS 600 External Layout, after [6].

b. REMUS Form Factor, Propulsion and Control Surfaces

The REMUS 600 is a torpedo-like form factor with a nose section, dry cylindrical pressure hulls and a tapered afterbody/tailcone assembly. The propulsor is a single open rotating propeller pushing the vehicle through the water from the aft end of the UUV. The control surfaces are shown in Figure 56, and are shown with more clarity in Figure 57.

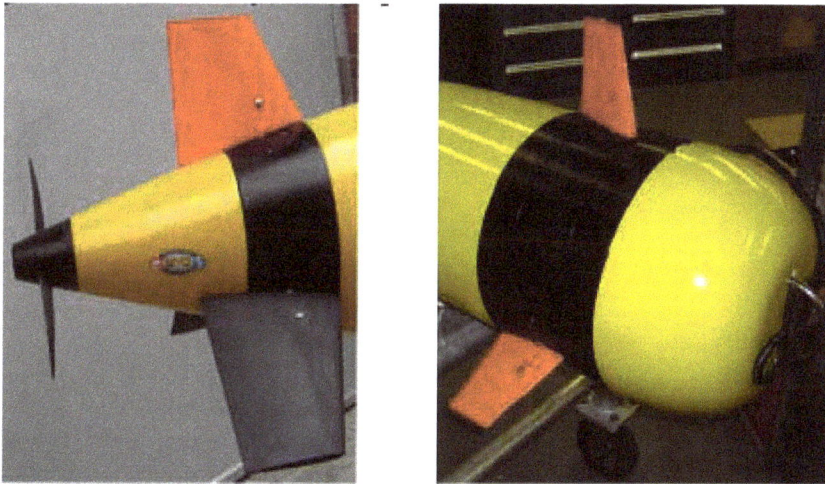

Figure 57.   REMUS 600's aft and forward control surface (fin) configuration, from [30].

As shown in [30], the aft control tri-fin assembly is an inverted "Y" configuration as is the optional forward tri-fin assembly. The control surfaces are "foiled" (i.e., a symmetric stretched tear drop) in cross section and controlled by independent actuators [6].

c. REMUS Energy

The REMUS 600 energy section is a self-contained hull section (see Battery/Electronics Section in Figure 56) that, according to [31], consists of 10 modules comprising a single lithium ion battery nominally at ~30V (volts). The capacity of the REMUS 600 battery system is 5.4 kilowatt-hour (kW-Hr) and is advertised to operate the

UUV continuously for seventy hours depending on the electrical load [6]. Figure 58, from [31], shows a typical REMUS 600 battery module and an assembled ten-module battery pack.

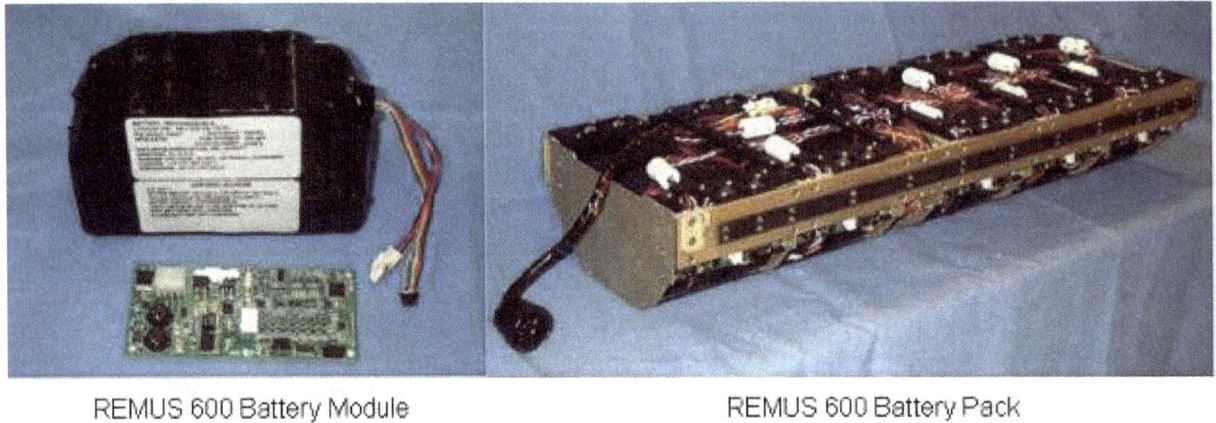

REMUS 600 Battery Module   REMUS 600 Battery Pack

Figure 58.   REMUS 600 Battery Module and Ten Module Battery Pack, after [31].

d.   *REMUS Pressure Hulls and Wet Volume*

The REMUS 600 hull sections are primarily dry pressure hulls, meaning the cylindrical sections are pressure hulls designed to withstand water pressure and maintain watertight integrity. When UUVs utilize right circular cylindrical pressure hulls, there is typically a "transition" of hull form on the ends of the cylinder. This transition is commonly a bulkhead with curvature, which leads to termination of the pressure volume. The REMUS 600 "caps" its pressure hulls on the forward end with a dry nose section (see Figure 56). The aft end of the pressure hull on the REMUS (Battery/Electronics Section in Figure 56) transitions utilizing a bulkhead down to its termination point in the steering assembly. Figure 59 shows the bulkhead aft of the battery section in a REMUS 600 and the transition "down" to another cylindrical sections which terminates (the pressure hull) inside the steering (fin) assembly. The smaller cylindrical section (looks like a pipe) allows dry cabling to pass into the steering assembly from the main sections of the UUV. This transition generates free-flood volume, which is utilized for "wet" sensors and hardware. The flooded section is "smoothed" with a fairing (also shown in Figure 59).

58

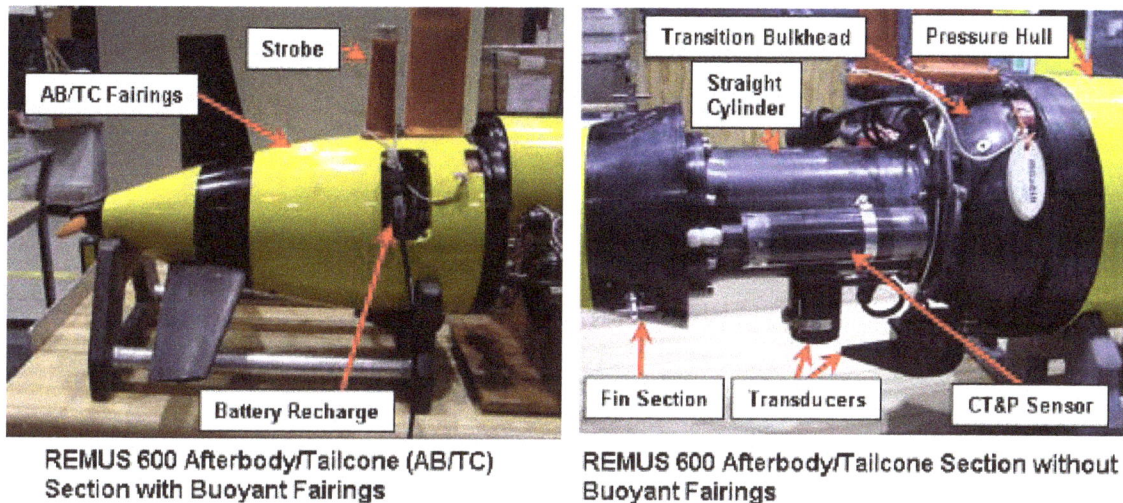

REMUS 600 Afterbody/Tailcone (AB/TC)
Section with Buoyant Fairings

REMUS 600 Afterbody/Tailcone Section without
Buoyant Fairings

Figure 59.   REMUS 600 Afterbody/Tail Assembly, after [32].

e.   *REMUS Sensors and Communications*

The sensors and communications of the REMUS 600 are almost entirely "exposed" to seawater, which is shown as commonplace among the UUV providers. Hydroid Inc's REMUS 600 brochure [6] lists standard and optional sensors, which are summarized in Table 1.

Standard	Optional
Acoustic Current Doppler Profiler (ADCP)	Dual Frequency Side Scan Sonar
Inertial Navigation Unit (INU)	Synthetic Aperture Sonar (SAS)
Side Scan Sonar (SSS)	Flourometers
Pressure	Acoustic Modem
Conductivity and Temperature (CT)	Video Camera
GPS	Acoustic Imaging
Iridium	Electronic Still Camera

Table 1.   REMUS 600 Standard and Optional Sensors, after [6].

Three of the sensors listed in Table 1 are related to communications; GPS, Iridium and Acoustic Modem. The GPS equipment (antenna and internal) on the UUV

59

receives (1-way) global positioning data from a satellite constellation for purposes of navigation. The Iridium equipment (antenna and internal) on the UUV is a 2-way, relatively low bandwidth, commercial satellite communication system. Both the GPS and Iridium require antennas that are above the surface of the water (i.e., when the UUV is floating on the surface). This is also the case for Wi-Fi radio frequency (RF) communications. It is shown that all providers selected for this analysis extend the GPS, Iridium and Wi-Fi antennas in the air in some manner when the UUV is surfaced. The REMUS has these airborne antennas on a fixed dorsal mast that is shown in Figure 56. The acoustic modem is a major component (along with transducers) in underwater communications. The modem in inboard of the UUV and the acoustic communication transducer is exposed to the seawater. The REMUS acoustic communications transducer is shown in Figure 56.

Six of the sensors listed in Table 1 are imaging systems. The four acoustic imaging systems; side scan sonar, dual frequency side scan sonar, synthetic aperture sonar and acoustic imaging, require the UUV architecture to directly "expose" the transducers to the seawater. The side-scan sonar transducer is shown in Figure 56 and there is one located on both sides (starboard and port) of the UUV. Two of the imaging sensors—video camera and electronic still camera—are based on optics and require that the camera lenses be directly exposed to seawater.

Three of the sensors listed in Table 1 measure physical properties of seawater: the conductivity and temperature sensor, the pressure sensor and the flourometer. These measurement sensors require exposure to seawater, but do not necessarily require a "line of sight" projecting away from the UUV like the communications and imagery sensors. The REMUS conductivity, temperature and pressure (CT&P) sensor is located in the aft free flood section (see Figure 59) and is enclosed by fairings during operation. The pressure sensor is simply exposed to the ambient pressure by residing in the free flood section. The conductivity and temperature sensors have a flow tube that penetrates a fairing to allow fresh and timely flow into the sensor for correlation. This tube ensures that stagnate water in the free flood is not used.

The remaining two sensors listed in Table 1 (ADCP and INU) aid in UUV navigation. The INU is internal to the UUV, or dry, but is aided by the seawater exposed ADCP transducers to retard system error growth. The ADCP is a set of four downward looking transducers located in the ADCP/INU Section of the REMUS (Figure 56).

All fourteen sensors discussed for the REMUS 600 impose architecture impacting considerations to the system. This is a common theme as other UUV systems are discussed. These drivers are based on required exposure to seawater and air. Only one sensor listed by Hydroid, the INU, does not require direct exposure to seawater or air, but the INU is aided by the GPS antenna (air exposure) and the ADCP's transducers (seawater exposure), which indicates an indirect consideration to air and water interface.

f.   REMUS Launch and Recovery

The REMUS 600 is a system that is launched and recovered on the surface. Included in this thesis is a discussion of a Hydroid and Woods Hole Oceanographic Institute's submerged cage launch and recovery (L&R) capability. It is also appropriate in this section to discuss the REMUS 6000 L&R, which is indicative of a more "ocean going" system comparable to other UUV architectures that are presented.

The REMUS 600 surface launch and recovery consists of a free-floating vehicle actively swimming off the surface and being recovered while drifting on the surface. Figure 60 shows recovery straps (lifting points) and nose recovery bails that are installed on the UUV. This equipment is kept on during operations and utilized for hook (i.e., crane, davit, etc…) based launch and recovery. The nose bail is shown in Figure 56 as well.

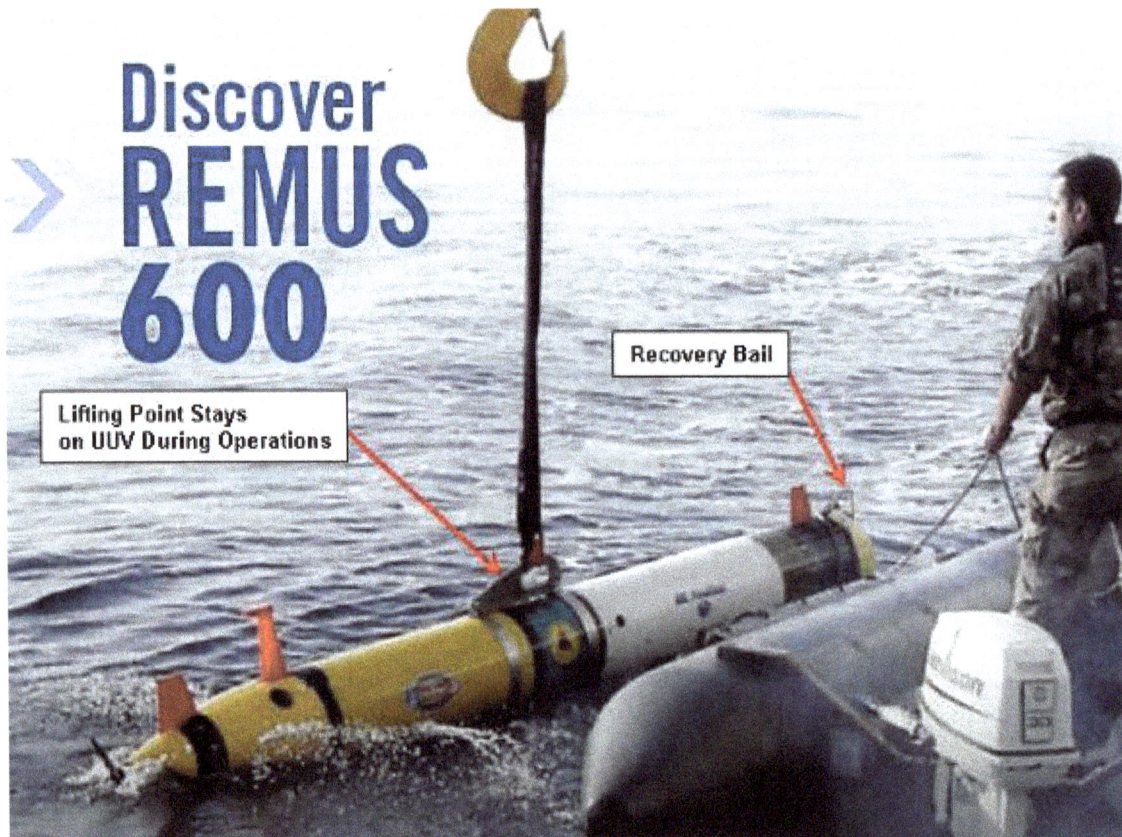

Figure 60.   REMUS 600 Launch and Recovery Technique, after [6].

This L&R method requires dexterity with equipment and manpower. The use of people very close (touching) to the vehicle, small boats and cantilevered hoists suggests quieter sea-state for safe and controlled L&R.

According to [33], to operate from ships of opportunity and to conduct L&R on larger ocean going ships a launch and recovery system (LARS) was developed for REMUS 600. Figure 61 shows the LARS for the REMUS 600. The shipboard recovery hardware utilizes typical ships interfaces (electric and hydraulic) and allows ocean-going operations. The LARS was demonstrated with REMUS 600 in sea-state 5 conditions. The recovery bail and main lifting point on the UUV are attached at sea by shipboard operators and a 30-foot carbon fiber pole.

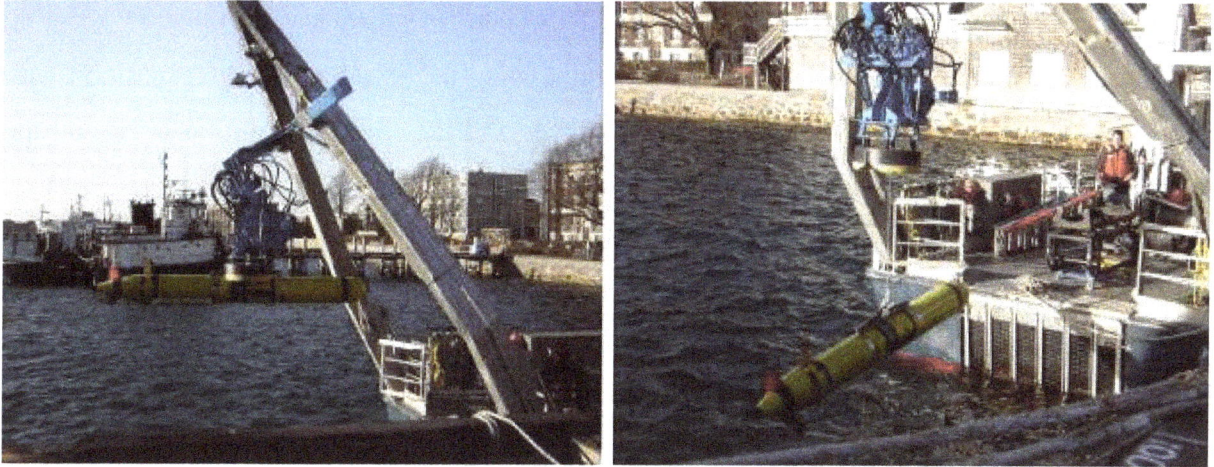

Figure 61.   REMUS 600 Launch and Recovery System (LARS), from [34].

The REMUS 6000 also has a LARS that eliminates the close proximity "pole hooking" that the REMUS 600 LARS utilizes. The REMUS 6000 LARS is shown in Figure 62.

Figure 62.   REMUS 6000 Launch and Recovery System (LARS), from [34].

According to [34], the REMUS 6000 LARS consists of the crew securing a UUV recovery line from a distance, manipulating the ship into a towing position with the UUV, and a winch operation that retrieves and lifts the UUV onto a cradle by the nose. The UUV releases a 36+ meter-long recovery line and float (from the nose) on command, which is captured with a grapple fired from a pneumatic gun as part of this process.

2. HUGIN 1000

a. HUGIN Layout

Layouts of the HUGIN 1000 are shown in Figures 63 and 64. Figure 63 is a simpler higher-level layout that highlights the major sections of the HUGIN; nose section, payload section, battery and payload transducer section, and the control and propulsion section.

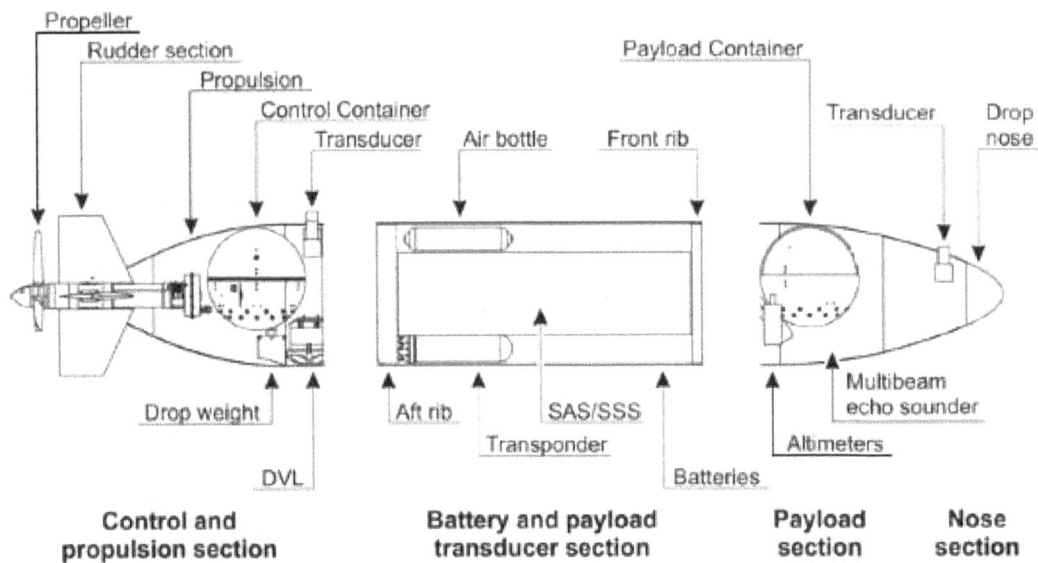

Figure 63.   HUGIN 1000 Layout, from [5].

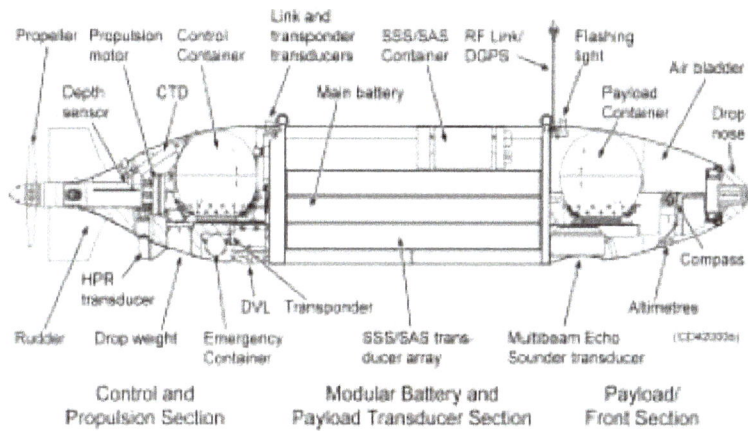

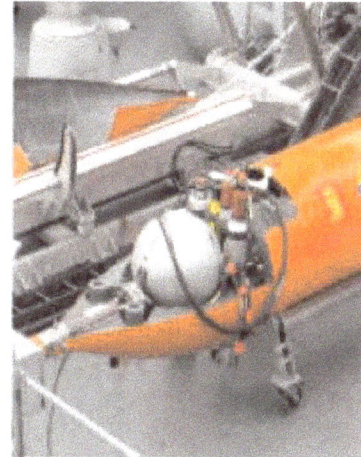

Figure 64.   HUGIN 1000 Layout, from [35].

Figure 64 shows better resolution of the HUGIN layout with locations of several components, sensors, and dry pressure spheres for payload and control hardware. Figure 65 shows a photo of the HUGIN 1000 with exposed hardware.

Figure 65.   HUGIN 1000 deployment, from [9].

b. *HUGIN Form Factor, Propulsion and Control Surfaces*

The HUGIN is a torpedo-like form factor UUV with a unique steep taper afterbody that leads to control surfaces and propulsor. The steep taper gives a "tear drop" characteristic to the HUGIN. The HUGIN has a single open propeller for propulsion and four control surfaces (fins) upstream of the propulsor. The propulsion section is shown in Figure 66 with an inset of a single control surface.

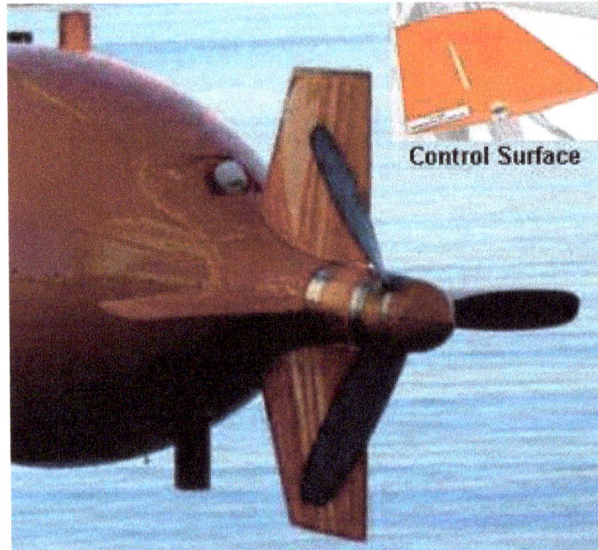

Figure 66.   HUGIN 1000 Propulsion System's Propeller and Control Surfaces, after [9].

c. *HUGIN Energy*

The HUGIN 1000's "standard" battery consists of three (3) modules comprising a single lithium polymer battery pack nominally at ~50V. Kongsberg opted for a 50V maximum system voltage to keep their battery system below the high voltage threshold and "non-hazardous." The capacity of the HUGIN battery is 15 kW-Hr and is advertised to operate the UUV continuously for twenty (20) hours based on an electrical load of 700W. The HUGIN battery is a pressure tolerant battery designed to operate at 1000 meters depth. According to [36], Kongsberg opted for a pressure tolerant system to eliminate the cost (in weight) of a deep diving battery section pressure hull. Figure 67 shows a typical HUGIN 1000 pressure tolerant lithium polymer battery.

Figure 67.   HUGIN 1000's pressure tolerant Lithium Polymer Battery, from [9].

d.   *HUGIN Pressure Hulls and Wet Volume*

The HUGIN 1000 is a flooded volume vehicle. Kongsberg's commitment to a pressure tolerant battery in the free-flood is a primary indicator of flooded volume architecture. Batteries are a significantly large and heavy component of the UUV system and utilizing pressure tolerant energy eliminates the need for dry and substantially large pressure vessels. The HUGIN layout in Figure 64 shows several components in the vehicle's free-flood region. The two large spheres, control container and payload container, in the HUGIN are the largest dry volumes dedicated to hardware. The right hand side photo in Figure 64 provides a good look at HUGIN's free flood anatomy. Figure 68 shows the payload and control containers utilized in HUGIN.

Figure 68.   HUGIN Payload and Control Containers Provide Dry Volume for UUV
Hardware, from [9].

e.   *HUGIN Sensors and Communications*

The HUGIN 1000 has several sensors and exposed communications equipment. Table 2 lists the common equipment offered by Kongsberg. All sensors in Table 2, except the CTD require exposure and "field of view" into the water. Similar to the REMUS, the HUGIN embeds the CTD underneath fairings and ports seawater in via plumbing for that sensor's operation.

Payload Specific	Communications Specific
Multi-Beam Echo-sounder (MBE)	Acoustic Communications Data Link
Side Scan Sonar (SSS)	Wi-Fi RF
Sub-Bottom Profiler (SBP)	Iridium
Synthetic Aperture Sonar (SAS)	Ethernet
Conductivity, Temperature & Density (CTD)	
Turbidity Sensor	
Acoustic Current Doppler Profiler (ADCP)	
Camera	

Table 2.   HUGIN 1000's Payload and Communications Equipment, after [9].

The hardware configuration and locations of most of the HUGIN's payload and communications sensors are shown in Figure 64 and Figure 69.

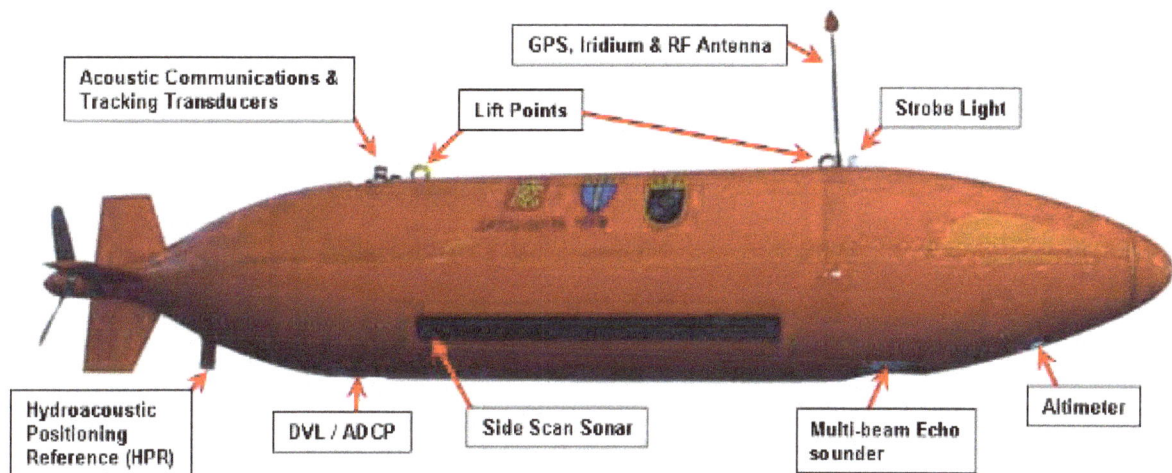

Figure 69.   HUGIN 1000 "Exposed" Sensors and Equipment, after [9].

f.   HUGIN Launch & Recovery

The HUGIN 1000 launch & recovery (L&R) is similar to the REMUS 6000 discussed in the previous section. From the surface, the positively buoyant HUGIN releases a recovery line and float from the nose when ready for recovery. Figure 70 shows the recovery sequence of the HUGIN from the surface ship.

Figure 70.   HUGIN Recovery Sequence, from [9].

For launch, the HUGIN is released and slides down (tail first) from the recovery cradle. Figure 71 shows a HUGIN launch from a surface ship (note: the nose is intact for launch).

Figure 71.   HUGIN Launch from Surface Ship, from [9].

3.   ISE Explorer

a.   *Explorer Layout*

Layouts of the ISE Explorer are shown in Figures 72 and 73. Figure 72 shows an exterior view of the Explorer with features called out. Similar to the other UUV systems the Explorer has several exterior or "exposed" sensors and hardware. The Explorer has a free-flood control bay (aft), a dry volume (pressure hull) in the middle, and a free-flood payload bay (forward).

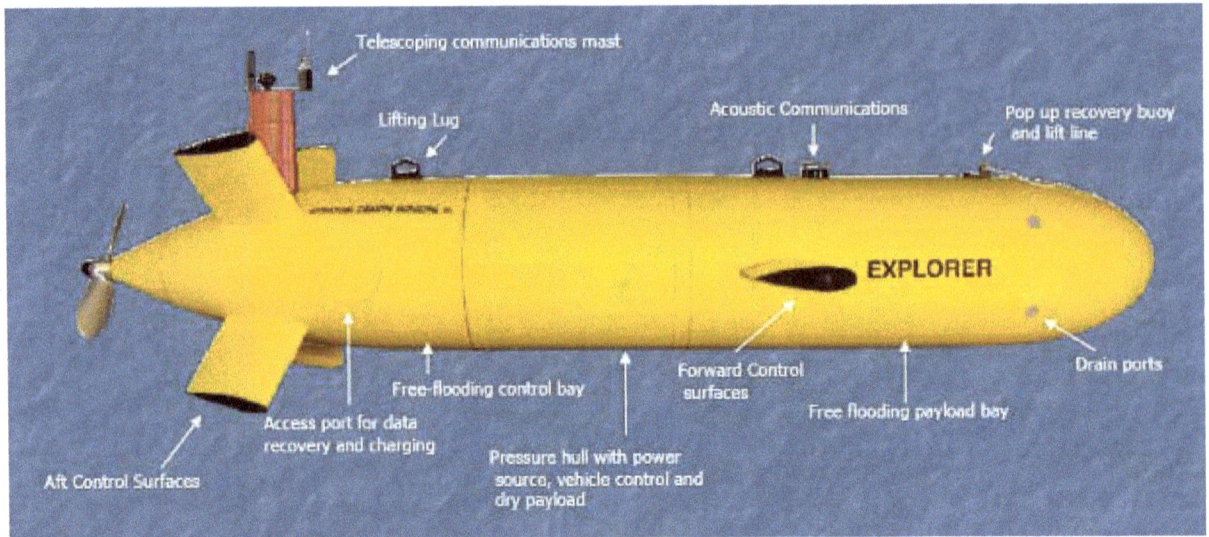

Figure 72.   Exterior View of ISE Explorer, from [37].

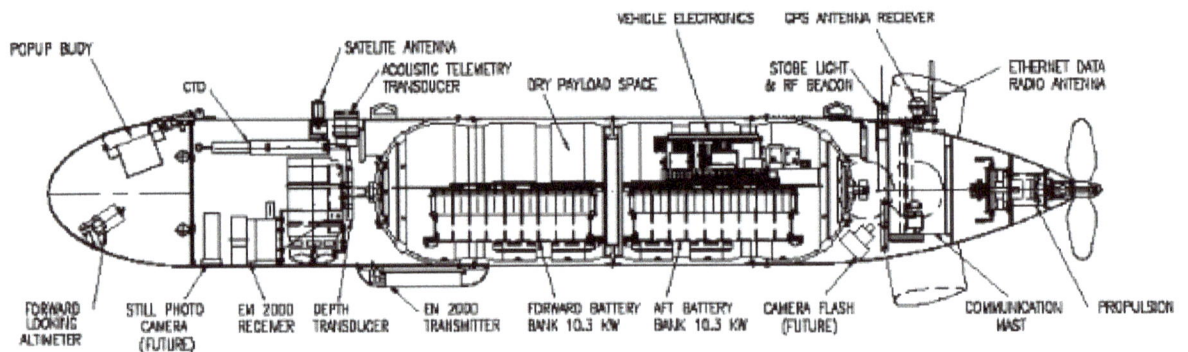

Figure 73.   Internal Layout of ISE Explorer, from [38].

The internal layout in Figure 73 more definitively shows the forward flooded payload bay, the dry pressure vessel for payload, and the aft flooded control bay. The forward bay is equipped with several sensors and components secured in the free-flood. The pressure vessel accommodates dry payload volume, two battery banks, and vehicle electronics. The aft control bay accommodates more sensors, the telescoping mast control surfaces and propulsion.

72

b. Explorer Form Factor, Propulsion and Control Surfaces

The Explorer form factor is also torpedo-like with a single open propeller for propulsion. There are six control surfaces (two horizontal forward canards and four aft on the afterbody) on the Explorer which are shown in Figure 74. The aft control surfaces (fins) are oriented in the "X" configuration and ISE located the telescoping mast (painted orange) at top-dead-center for surface communications.

Figure 74.   Explorer's Control Surfaces and Propulsor, from [11].

c. Explorer Energy

According to [39] and [40], the Explorer battery is based on 1.6 kW-Hr modules that comprise the three bank 48 kW-Hr lithium ion battery that nominally operates at ~48V. Two battery banks are shown in the dry volume pressure vessel in Figure 73. The Explorer can operate continuously for 36 hours in the 48 kW-Hr battery configuration [38].

d. Explorer Pressure Hulls and Wet Volume

The Explorer is unique compared to the other UUVs being presented in terms of free flood and dry volume. All other vehicles being discussed have a "dominant" dry or wet volume configuration, but Explorer, has a more "balanced" dry/wet volume ratio. Figure 73 shows the pressure vessel in the center portion of the UUV where batteries, dry payload and vehicle electronics are located. The pressure vessel is cylindrical with bulkheads on either end.

e. Explorer Sensors and Communications

The ISE Explorer has several sensors and exposed communications equipment consistent with the other UUV's being discussed. Table 3 lists the common equipment offered by ISE. The Explorer is the first UUV discussed with a telescoping mast that dynamically extends and retracts into the UUV whereas the other systems utilize fixed rigid masts. The mast is dedicated to airborne communication equipment: GPS antenna, Wi-Fi radio, strobe light and RF beacon. The mast is shown well in Figure 72. An interesting note is that the satellite antenna is on the main body of the vehicle (see Figure 73) and not on the mast where is seems most sensible, it is not clear whether that antenna is for typical communications (i.e., Iridium) or a satellite based emergency locator. The camera equipment and multi-beam echo sounder are downward facing units in the free-flood and shown in Figure 73. The CTD and depth sensor are "embedded" in the free-flood and do not need "line of sight" into the seawater. These are also shown in Figure 73.

Payload Specific	Communications Specific
Multi-Beam Echo-sounder (EM-200) MBE	Acoustic Communications Data Link
Dual Frequency Side Scan Sonar	Wi-Fi
Sub-Bottom Profiler (SBP)	Iridium
Magnetometer	
Conductivity, Temperature & Density (CTD)	
Depth Sensor	
Camera	

Table 3.   ISE Explorer Payload Sensors and Communications Equipment, after [40, 41, 38].

f.   *Explorer Launch & Recovery*

The launch and recovery of the Explorer is not as extensively documented as other UUV systems discussed. According to [41], the Explorer has a pop-up buoy and line mechanism called the "line-locker." The locker deploys ~30 meters of line (on command) connected to a float to aid recovery. The Explorer also utilizes floodable ballast tanks (~50 kg of water) to "park" the UUV on the bottom and a drop weight (~90 kg) that is acoustically released to support a "park and recover later" CONOP. Figure 75 shows a variable ballast tank and drop weight. Figures 72 and 73 show the pop-up recovery buoy sub-system in the nose section.

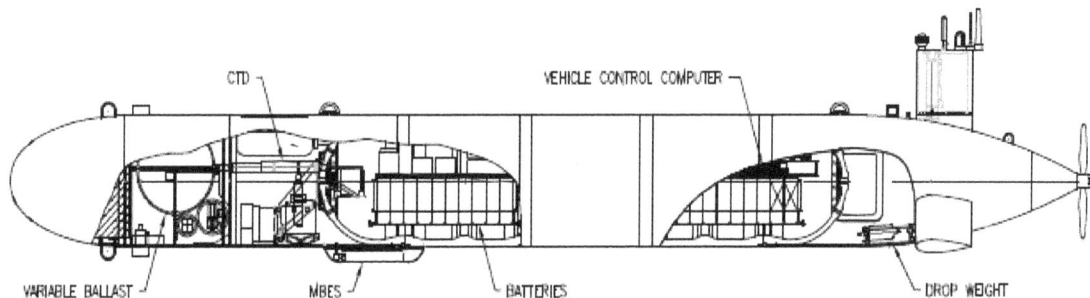

Figure 75.   Explorer's Ballast Tanks and Drop Weight Aid L&R Operations, from [40].

4.   Bluefin-12

a.   Bluefin-12 Layout

Figure 76 shows a layout of Bluefin Robotics Inc's Bluefin-12. According to [42], the UUV consists of two major sections: payload section and tail-cone section. Figure 77 shows a layout of the Bluefin-12 with integrated synthetic aperture sonar (SAS). Although Figure 77 is not a standard or stock configuration of Bluefin-12, it effectively shows several of the core Bluefin-12 components in layout.

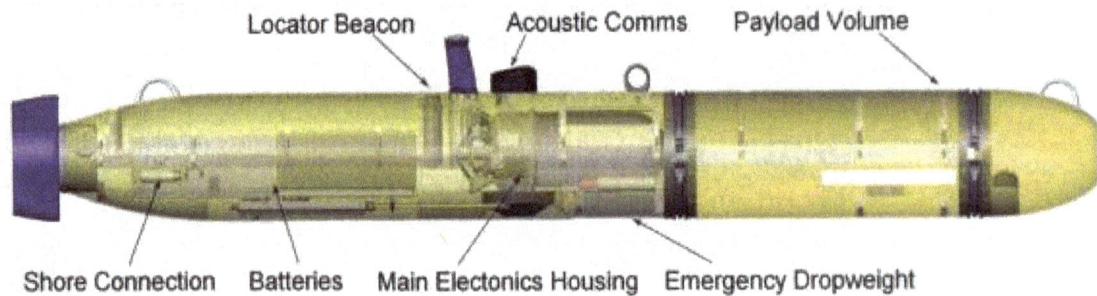

Figure 76.   Layout of Bluefin Robotics Inc's Bluefin-12, from [16].

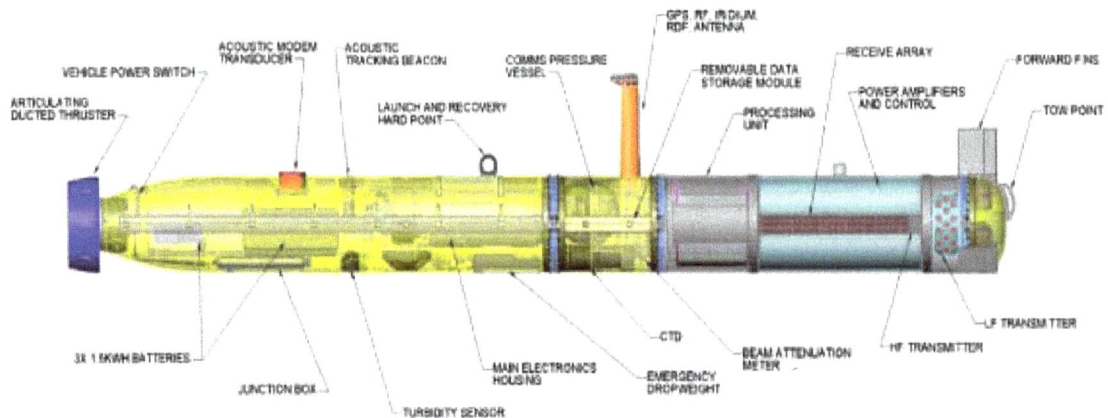

Figure 77.   Layout of Bluefin Robotics Inc's Bluefin-12 with a Synthetic Aperture Sonar Integrated, from [43].

76

b. Bluefin-12 Form Factor, Propulsion and Control Surfaces

The Bluefin-12 is also a torpedo-like form factor. There is a unique difference in the Bluefin-12 control and propulsion architecture that is substantially different from the other UUVs being discussed, in that the Bluefin-12 does not (typically) have any active control surfaces (i.e., fins). The dynamic control of the Bluefin-12 is induced by an articulating ducted thruster on the aft end of the UUV (called out in Figure 77). Figure 78 shows the aft-end layout of Bluefin-12 and offers an informative view of the unique propulsion system.

Figure 78.   Bluefin-12 Aft-End Layout, after [44].

Figure 79 shows and end view of the Bluefin-12 propulsor. The propulsor is ducted with a single rotating rotor (i.e., propeller). The duct (or shroud) is secured in space by stators (fixed vanes) that are upstream of the rotor. The articulation of the tailcone "vectors" the thrust and dynamic response of the UUV. It is not apparent that this thruster offers any vehicle "roll" control; this leads to the conclusion that the Bluefin-12 must statically trim (i.e., the center of gravity below the center of buoyancy) the vehicle to create a righting force or pull-around in the roll plane.

Figure 79.   Bluefin-12's Propulsor, from [45].

c.   ***Bluefin-12 Energy***

The Bluefin-12 utilizes a "wet" pressure tolerant lithium polymer battery. The battery is comprised of three 1.5 kW-Hr modules [46] that are nominally 32V [42]. Figure 80 shows the 1.5 kW-Hr module from Bluefin Robotics Inc.

Figure 80.   Bluefin Robotics Inc's Pressure Tolerant 1.5 kW-hr
32-Volt Battery Module used in Bluefin-12, from [46].

According to [16], with three battery modules in Bluefin-12 (4.5 kW-Hr), the vehicle is capable of approximately twenty hours of continuous information. Figure 78 shows the three battery modules assembled in the Bluefin-12.

d.   Bluefin-12 Pressure Hulls and Wet Volume

As already eluded to from previous discussion and figures, the Bluefin-12 is a free-flood UUV system. The layouts (Figures 76 and 77) show the flooded architecture. As indicated in [42], foam is used extensively in the Bluefin-12 for purposes of mounting, packaging and floatation. Figure 78 (above) shows the free flood nature of the Bluefin-12's architecture and not only highlights the individual pressure tolerant components (i.e., main electronics housing, transducers, batteries and propulsor module) but also shows the foam packaging methods used around various components in the vehicle.

e.   Bluefin-12 Sensors and Communications

Common Bluefin-12 sensors and communications hardware is listed in Table 4.

Payload Specific	Communications Specific
Synthetic Aperture Sonar (SAS)	Acoustic Communications
Side Scan Sonar (SSS)	Wi-Fi (RF) & Ethernet
Buried Object Scanning Sonar (BOSS)	Iridium Satellite Communications
Gradiometer (i.e magnetometer)	GPS Receive
Conductivity, Temperature & Density (CTD)	
Forward Look Sonar (FLS)	
Turbidity Sensor	

Table 4.   Bluefin-12 Sensors and Communications Hardware Offered by Bluefin Robotics Inc., after [47, 43].

The buried object scanning sonar is not a "typical" application and is being developed by the US Navy for mine countermeasures (MCM) use. The other sensors and communication related hardware are typical to the other UUVs being presented. The CTD and turbidity sensor are shown in the translucent layout in Figure 77. The turbidity sensor is mounted for "line of sight" into the surrounding water column. The CTD sensor is embedded in the flooded region of the UUV. No imaging sonars are pictured here in this discussion. The fixed rigid mast houses the RF antennas (Wi-Fi & beacon), GPS receive antenna, and the Iridium satellite communications antenna. Two different versions of the mast are shown in Figures 77 and 78. The acoustic communications transducer is shown at top-dead-center of the Bluefin-12 in Figure 78. The acoustic tracking transducer is shown in Figure 77, which is mounted on top-dead-center of the UUV.

f. *Bluefin-12 Launch & Recovery*

There was not substantial information found specifically on Bluefin-12 launch and recovery (L&R). There are several launch and recovery methods discussed in [16], but typically, it is apparent that the Bluefin-12 is launched and recovered from the surface with lifting capability provided by the support craft. The layout in Figure 77 shows hardware integrated into the UUV that supports L&R including launch and recovery hard point, emergency drop weight, and forward tow point. Figure 81 shows the Bluefin-12 operating at the surface and Figure 82 shows the UUV on the deck of its support craft. Other photos found in references show the Bluefin-12 on open deck support crafts supported by A-frame lifting equipment as well.

Figure 81.   Bluefin-12 Operating at the Surface, from [15].

Figure 82.   Bluefin-12 on Deck of Operations Craft, from [47].

5.   Hafmynd Gavia

a.   *Gavia Layout*

The external layout of Hafmynd's Gavia Scientific is shown in Figure 83. The Gavia consists of modules consisting of Propulsion, Control, Geo-Swath, INS/DVL, Battery and Nose.

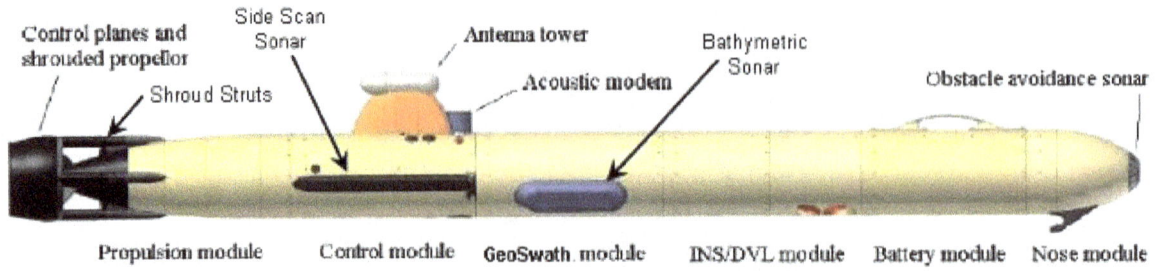

Figure 83.   External Layout of Hafmynd's Gavia Scientific, after [48].

b.   *Gavia Form Factor, Propulsion and Control Surfaces*

The Gavia form factor is torpedo-like with a relatively high length to diameter ratio. The ducted propulsor and control surfaces are shown in Figure 83 and more closely in Figure 84.

Figure 84.   Gavia's Propulsor, from [49].

The propuslor consists of a single rotating rotor (i.e., propeller) that is shrouded by a duct and upstream of the control surfaces (moving fins). The shroud is supported by four struts that connect the shroud to the UUV body and are shown well in Figure 83. This propulsor is unique to the other UUV in this discussion. This is the only propulsor that has the control surfaces not only surrounded by the propulsor duct, but also in the propeller "exhaust" or wake of the propeller.

c.   *Gavia Energy*

The Gavia is typically equipped with a single 1.2 kW-Hr lithium ion battery [50] that can operate the Gavia for 6-15 hours (depending on electrical load) [51]. The Gavia battery module hull section serves as the container/enclosure for the cells. The module also has its own internal PC controls for charging management [51]. Figure 85 shows the Gavia 1.2 kW-Hr battery module. The voltage of the Gavia battery was not found.

Figure 85.   Gavia Single 1.2 kW-Hr battery module, from [51].

d.   *Gavia Pressure Hulls and Wet Volume*

The Gavia has completely dry pressure hull architecture, unlike the other UUVs being discussed. The pressure hulls share a common joint so they can be interchanged or replaced in a modular manner. Figure 86 shows the Gavia pressure hulls and a typical installation (or removal) of the nose section from the vehicle.

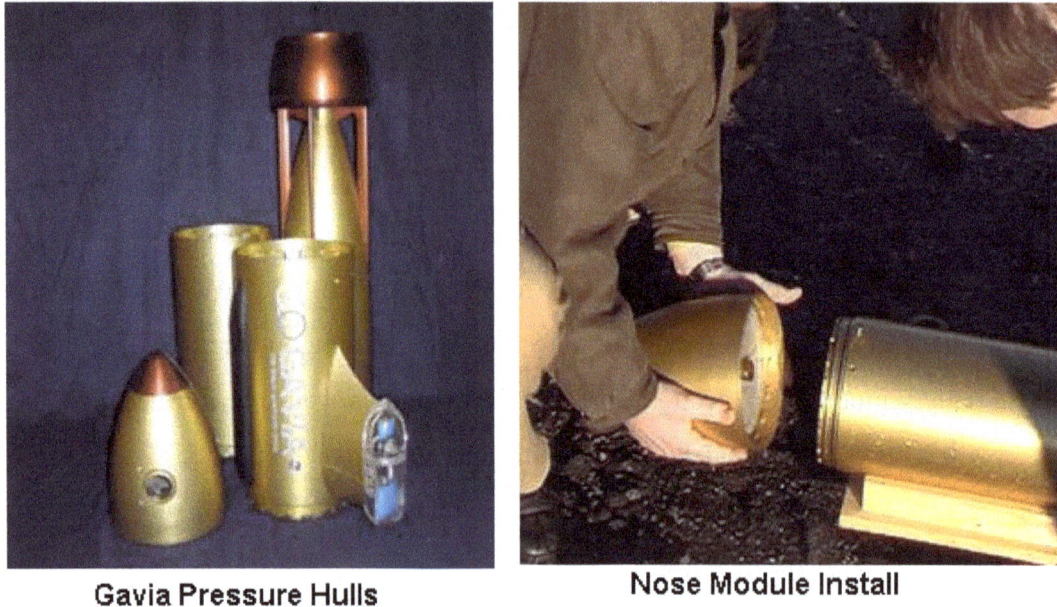

Gavia Pressure Hulls   Nose Module Install

Figure 86.   Gavia Pressures Hulls, after [47].

e.   *Gavia Sensors and Communications*

The Gavia is a relatively well-equipped UUV considering its size compared to the other UUVs being discussed. Table 5 lists the sensors and communications hardware offered by Hafmynd for the Gavia Scientific.

Payload Specific	Communications Specific
Bathymetric Sonar (Geo-Swath)	Acoustic Communications
Dual Frequency Side Scan Sonar (SSS)	Wi-Fi (RF) & Ethernet
Conductivity, Temperature & Density (CTD)	Iridium Satellite Communications
Forward Look Sonar (FLS)	GPS Receive
Camera with Lighting Strobe	

Table 5.   Gavia's Sensors and Communications Equipment Offered, after [52].

The control section of the Gavia (see Figure 83) contains all communications equipment listed in Table 5 as well as the side scan sonar, CTD, emergency transducer and camera strobe. The GeoSwath section contains is an optional module that contains the bathymetric and backscatter transducer. The nose section contains the forward-looking sonar. Most sensors are exposed, similar to the other UUVs.

f.   Gavia Launch & Recovery

The Gavia is considered "man-portable" for launch and recovery operations. The battery section has a handle for operator use during launch and recovery (Figure 83). The base Gavia's weight in air is ~49 kg (108 lbs) [50] and is more realistically "two-man portable." Figure 87 and Figure 88 both show launch and recovery operations with multiple operators. Figure 87 shows recovery fixtures (slings) being utilized.

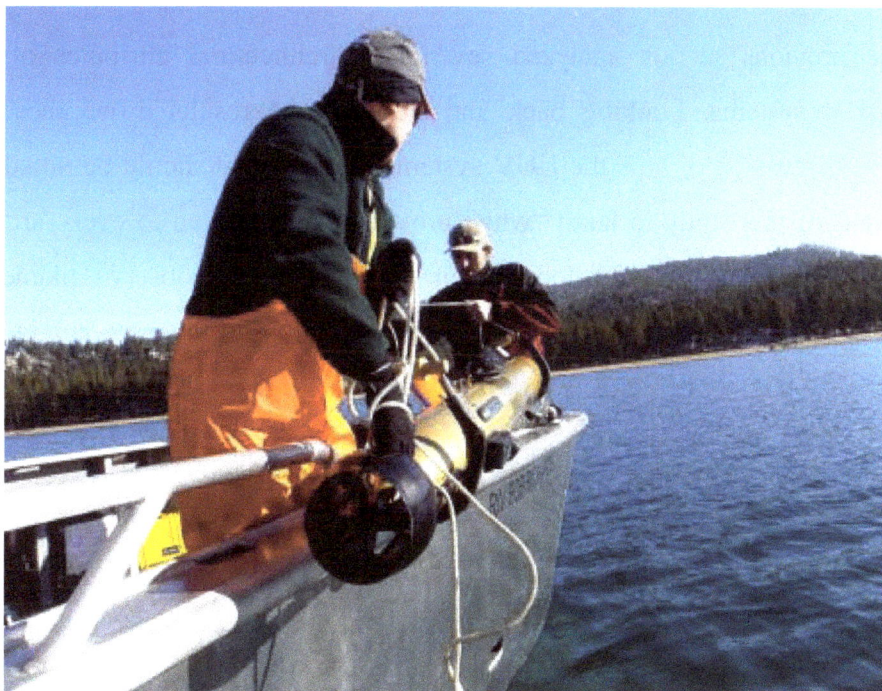

Figure 87.   Gavia 2-Man Launch & Recovery, from [49].

Figure 88.   Gavia Military Recovery, from [50].

C.   COMPARISON, SUMMARY AND DISCUSSION OF KEY ARCHITECTURAL ATTRIBUTES

The previous section analyzed seven key architectural attributes of the five selected UUV systems. Looking back and studying the results drove the following comparative discussion of how the UUV systems compared. It should be noted that it is not the intent of this study to learn "why" providers were driven to every architectural design decision when they developed their systems, but to observe likenesses and differences in these attributes, identify trends and propose potential driving considerations the system architects may have considered during development.

1.   Form Factor, Propulsion and Control Surfaces

Table 6 shows a quick summary of the form factor, propulsion and control surfaces discussion.

UUV System	Form Factor	Propulsion	Control Surfaces
REMUS 600	Torpedo-Like	Single Open Propeller	Aft Tri-Fin (inverted Y) Upstream of Propeller
HUGIN 1000	Torpedo-Like	Single Open Propeller	Aft Quad-Fin (+) Upstream of Propeller
Explorer	Torpedo-Like	Single Open Propeller	Aft Quad-Fin (X)
Bluefin-12	Torpedo-Like	Single Shrouded Propeller	No Fins. Articulating Shrouded Propeller
Gavia Scientific	Torpedo-Like	Single Shrouded Propeller	Quad-fin (+) Downstream of Propulsor

Table 6.   Summary of form factor, propulsion and control surfaces.

All the UUV systems were torpedo-like in main body shape. There were other UUV's researched in the survey in Chapter II that had non-traditional (non-torpedo) shapes, but the selected systems (successful in the marketplace) maintain the relatively low drag faired (and symmetrical) torpedo hydrodynamic shape with a single propulsor that accepts (i.e., the propulsor inlet) the trailing flow from the main body. It is interesting to note that the torpedo like shape is conducive to architectures with strictly pressure hulls (Gavia), strictly free-flooding volume (Bluefin-12) and hybrid combinations of both (ISE Explorer). One conclusion drawn is the faired traditional shapes prevail and different structural and water integrity preferences (dry versus free-flood) can both be adapted.

The propulsion for the selected UUV's varied to a small degree. The REMUS, HUGIN and Explorer, all with open single propellers, have propellers with two, three and two blades, respectively. The propellers are all similar to typical pleasure craft (boats) propellers and are not indicative of any highly efficient propeller. A conclusion drawn here is these providers chose very simple (likely commercially available) propellers. Only higher power and higher speed objectives would likely put a premium on propulsor efficiency. The Bluefin and Gavia shrouded their single propellers (each with three blades). Potential considerations that drove this difference: safety concerns with exposed propellers, more hydrodynamic efficiency and thrust controlling the flow at the blade tips with the shroud (i.e., according to [53], a more efficient "nozzle" effect), and less chance of entanglement with debris, nets, ropes, etc… As mentioned earlier, it is not the scope of this thesis to research every architectural design decision, but to propose likely considerations made.

The control surface configurations were of significant difference in a few respects. The REMUS, HUGIN and Explorer all had control surfaces (i.e., moving fins) extruding beyond the diameter of the vehicle's main body, located on the afterbody and upstream of the propulsor. The notable item looking at these three systems in their basic configurations is; the REMUS has one less control surface (3 versus 4) than Explorer or HUGIN. The system (or sub-system) designer would need to consider the trade between minimum fin area required for positive authority to control the vehicle and available actuator (or servo) capabilities, properties and powering requirements. Fewer control surfaces are a distinct advantage in many ways if the system level engineering trades would support this attribute.

The Explorer has two forward control surfaces as "standard" and the REMUS has three forward control surfaces as "optional." This attribute could be driven by the UUV's requirement for slower speed with fin authority, a harsher operating environment such as the surf zone or possibly a requirement to swim with external pods, extensions or "bumps" that would stress vehicle hydrodynamic control. Thorough system requirements with regards to the vehicle speed, size and operating environment are extremely important to the system architect. The ability to "expand" vehicle control with additional fin area is desirable and gives more capability to the UUV system.

An interesting feature of the Explorer is that the control surfaces appear proportionally large compared to the other UUVs presented. Their size driver is unknown; possibly the considerations or driving requirements mentioned above may explain their fairly prominent proportions. Another potential explanation is ISE's other (and much larger) UUV platform "Theseus" may have offered ancestry and presented ISE designers with cost savings (another systems engineering trade consideration) by leveraging legacy control surface assets, infrastructure, etc.

The Bluefin-12 vehicle control method (by articulating the thruster) is clearly unlike the other vehicles presented. As discussed with its presentation in the previous section, there is not a "roll control" capability to this propulsor other than static heel with ballast or an exposed trim tab (both optimized for a single speed). This stresses (again) the need for careful consideration-to and development-of requirements and their potential growth. A new sensor, for example, may come with a very stringent stability requirement in the roll plane or the vehicle CONOP may call for abrupt speed changes which could cause vacillation in vehicle roll (i.e., from changes of propulsor torque on the UUV). Engineering considerations and trade-studies of this propulsor would consider roll effects, propulsor effectiveness, simplicity of design, benefits of having no fins, etc.

Finally, with regards to the control surface discussion…the Gavia is another different control system, which partly explains its inclusion in this thesis. The control surfaces on the Gavia are immediately downstream of the propeller and surrounded by the propulsor shroud. These are interpreted as valuable attributes if the engineering trades would support them at a more system level. First, as indicated in [54], a dominant contributor to the force on a control surface is the velocity of the water passing over it; in fact, it is the mathematical square of the velocity (V^2). The flow immediately aft (i.e., in the wake) of the propeller in a duct is significantly accelerated compared to the velocity of the vehicle. This means that the effectiveness of the control surface in the propeller wake is greater than if it were upstream of the propeller in the vehicle flow. Second, the control surfaces are less likely to be fouled, damaged or entangled being "contained" in the shroud. Considerations the architect would face include complexity of integrating the fins in the shroud, complexity of actuating the fins in the shroud, maintenance and access issues, etc.

Figure 89 shows the Naval Oceanographic Office's (NAVOCEANO) Seahorse AUV. The Seahorse has a ducted propeller and the control surfaces (in the X-configuration) are in the immediate wake of the propeller. This is similar to the Gavia propulsor at a much larger scale.

Figure 89.   NAVOCEANO's Seahorse with a ducted propulsor and control surfaces in the propeller wake from [55]. The inset photo, from [1] shows the rotating blade row.

2.   Energy Systems

The UUV energy systems discussed are summarized in Table 7. After the discussion of battery chemistries in Chapter III, lithium-based seemed to offer the appealing solution for UUVs since they are energy dense and lightweight. All UUVs analyzed in this chapter selected a lithium secondary (i.e., rechargeable) battery to integrate into their vehicle architecture.

UUV System	Energy Chemistry	System Approx. Voltage	Capacity
REMUS 600	Lithium-Ion	~30V	5.4 kW-Hr
HUGIN 1000	Lithium-Polymer	~50V	15.0 kW-Hr
Explorer	Lithium-Ion	~48V	48.0 kW-Hr
Bluefin-12	Lithium-Polymer	~32V	4.5 kW-Hr
Gavia Scientific	Lithium-Ion	Unknown	1.2 kW-Hr

Table 7.   Summary of Energy Characteristics.

The batteries offered by the five UUV providers were all "expandable" by putting another "pack" or "module" in parallel into the UUV. The providers were all quick to offer (advertise) growth in endurance, range, etc. by doing this. It was difficult to clearly differentiate which system had more endurance or continuous operations since they all advertised with different assumptions on what the load on the system actually was. The HUGIN for example, advertises its endurance as 24 hours at 4 knots with a load of over 700W that includes the multi-beam echo sounder, side scan sonar, sub-bottom profiler and CTD meter all operating (according to [9]). Others, such as the Bluefin-12 offer a range of endurance dependant on load (i.e., vehicle speed) of 10-23 hours of operation, according to [43]. With similar chemistries, the size of the battery can be gauged for all these UUVs by looking at their total electrical capacity (right-hand column of Table 7).

With a premium and finite limit on energy onboard a UUV, a major architectural consideration is the conservation and management of energy. The following considerations by the system architect warrant careful analysis to help maximize the UUVs on-station or operational time:

- When and how long to activate sensors, payloads and associated equipment. This could include on-board processing, active sensors, data recording, etc.

- Minimizing baseline or hotel UUV systems energy consumption. This could include propulsion loads, vehicle control, communications, navigation techniques, etc.

- Managing the operational planning. This could include time and locations to deploy (considering tides and currents), adaptive path planning to minimize transit times, mission planning such as when and how often to dwell, drift, communicate, bottom, transit, etc.

The last energy consideration an architect must consider (for this discussion anyway) is approvals and certifications required to store, use, transport, charge, discharge, access and essentially "operate" lithium batteries. They are a hazardous material and highly energetic with a reputation for fire incidents. To be able to build a UUV system that can be used in the commercial or military sector effectively with a relatively large lithium battery energy source is likely a substantial challenge.

3. Pressure Hulls and Wet Volume

The UUVs selected for analysis utilize both wet volume and dry (pressure vessel) volume. Table 8 shows a summary of "preference" of UUV providers with regards to internal vehicle volumes.

UUV System	Typical Depth Rating (m)	Mostly Dry Volume	Mostly Flooded Volume	Combination of Dry & Flooded
REMUS 600	600	X		
HUGIN 1000	1000		X	
Explorer	3000			X
Bluefin-12	1500		X	
Gavia Scientific	500	X		

Table 8.   Summary of Provider Preferences for UUV Internal Volumes.

All UUVs investigated (Chapter II) utilize some dry volumes to safeguard components from seawater and its associated pressure. "Mostly flooded volume" UUV architecture is one that has relatively small and individual pressure vessels distributed in significant flooded volume in the internal space. "Mostly dry volume" UUV architecture is one that has one (or few) relatively large dry volume (i.e., pressure hull) that is designed for accommodating multiple dry components. The discussion of wet and dry volumes in Chapter III focused on generalizations of depth, material, buoyancy, structure and access. Now with a better understanding of the five UUV systems, the architectural considerations are revisited. System architects should consider the advantages and disadvantages of both design philosophies. Below a few key pros (+) and cons (-) of each are discussed.

Architectural Considerations of Large Dry Volumes:

+ Allows integration of substantial unprotected hardware and components. Conducive to operation of bread-boards, developmental systems, new systems, etc… that have not been "packaged" for ocean environment.

+ Dry cabling of these internal components is less expensive and more flexible than wet cables.

+ More (shore-side) flexibility at less expense. The internal volume permits relatively easy maneuvering and manipulation of components.

- Larger volumes expected to withstand significant external pressure loads are structurally complex. This can drive expensive materials to combat weight and large seals/glands to contend with water integrity, and more complex manufacturing/machining processes; all of which drive costs. Penetrations for cables, plumbing, etc…would also add structural and manufacturing complexity.

- Large volumes may be more difficult to access in the field, especially if the pressure hull is integral to the overall system structure. Opening a large volume in a harsh (i.e., salt and humidity) environment may not be desirable or practical. Accessing a large volume would require time consuming processes (i.e., evacuation and backfill) to prepare it for re-entry to the water.

- Large internal dry volumes with electronics could cause heat problems.

Of the five UUVs analyzed, there was not a preference towards "wet" or "dry" (as is indicated in Table 8). There clearly has been success in the market place with each. A designer may conclude there is a factor or "preference" for the architecture in terms of wet or dry philosophies. Preference would be guided by how important the different pros and cons are with respect to requirements, CONOPS, etc., to the architect.

Architectural Considerations of Wet Volume:

+ More conducive to deeper depth capability. Small pressure vessels, waterproof (or oil filled) cabling, and utilization of pressure rated foam (i.e., syntactic foam) are indicative of deep diving systems. When considering the different UUVs in Chapter II; the deep divers typically utilize the "mostly flooded volume" philosophy. The issues (i.e., cons) with large pressure vessels escalate with deeper depths. Deep diving remotely operated vehicles (ROV) also utilize spheres, pressure tolerant oil filled cables and pressure tolerant buoyancy devices.

+ Many sensors utilized by UUVs are pre-packaged and available for flooded environments. Multiple sensors and devices presented in this chapter are "ready" for free-flooded regions.

+ Access and maintenance in the field. Free flood architectures can be accessed (typically) more easily and with less vulnerability than large pressure volumes.

- Less flexibility for developmental systems. Developmental systems are typically not designed for wet volumes.

- Issues with wet cabling. Wet or oil-filled cables are heavy, expensive, have long lead times for delivery, and require careful handling and maintenance.

- Difficulty achieving buoyancy. Small pressure volumes and large flooded regions make positive buoyancy difficult to achieve compared to vehicles with large air filled volumes.

An additional "free flood dominant" UUV architecture is the Boeing Echo Ranger (see Figure 49). The Echo Ranger and the ISE Explorer both favor free-flood design but are "forced" to make their dry volume pressure vessels larger to accommodate (relatively large) dry batteries. The Echo Ranger layout is shown in Figure 90 where the larger dry volume in the free-flood architecture is called out. Table 8 lists the Explorer as a "combination" of wet/dry preference, but if pressure tolerant batteries were used, the Explorer would likely be a free flood dominant design.

Free flood systems like the HUGIN 1000 and the Bluefin-12 that have pressure tolerant (wet) batteries do not require such a large pressure vessel like the Echo Ranger and Explorer systems.

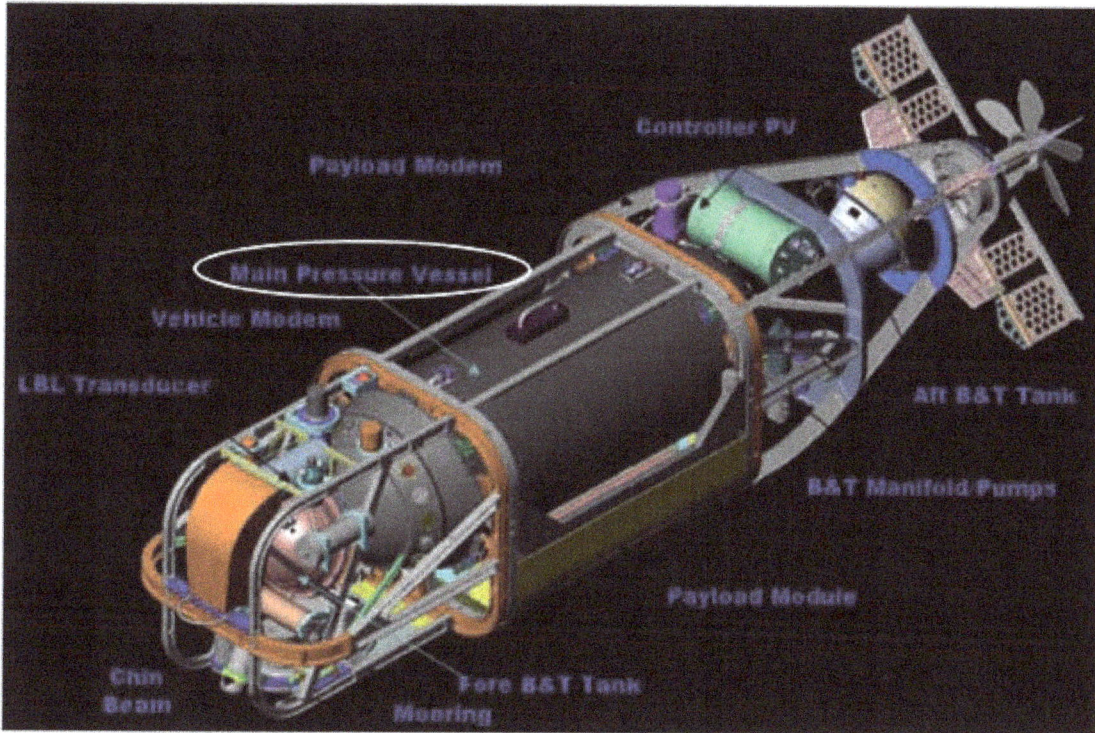

Figure 90.   Boeing's Echo Ranger System Layout Shows the Larger Main Pressure
Vessel that Accommodates Dry Batteries, after [56].

4.   Sensors and Communications

The first discussion of sensors and communications (Chapter III) spoke generally regarding location, vulnerability, orientation and antenna height. After consideration of the five UUVs, there was notable commonality in "what" type of sensors were integrated onto the platforms and some differences in "how" the sensors and communications hardware was integrated into the UUV. Table 9 shows a summary of most sensors and communications equipment discussed for the five UUVs.

UUV System	Communications				Sensors								
	GPS Receiver	Ethernet Wi-Fi (RF)	Irridium SATCOM	Acoustic Communi cations	Side Scan Sonar	Muliti-beam Echo Sounder	Synthetic Aperture Sonar	Bathymetric Sonar	Cameras	Conducti vity, Temperat ure & Density	Turbidity	Magnet ometer	Sub-Bottom Profiler
REMUS 600	X	X	X	X	X		X	X	X	X			
HUGIN 1000	X	X	X	X	X	X	X		X	X	X		X
Explorer	X	X	X	X	X	X	X		X	X	X	X	X
Bluefin-12	X	X	X	X	X					X		X	X
Gavia Scientific	X	X	X	X	X			X	X	X			

Table 9.   Summary of UUV Communications and Sensor Availability.

The communications portion of Table 9 is a complete set in terms of commonality. All UUVs utilize these communications systems. This trend points an architect towards a communications suite of GPS receive (for navigation), RF Wi-Fi (short-range wireless), Iridium (satellite communications) and underwater acoustic communications. The communications capability with these (above) components are considered baseline to vehicle operations.

The sensors portion of Table 9 indicates a couple of strong trends and an array of "experienced" sensors for use that should be affiliated with mission desires (requirements) and not necessarily vehicle baseline hardware. The side-scan sonar (SSS) and conductivity, temperature and density (CTD) sensors are common to the five UUVs and may indicate a baseline vehicle sensor capability (to measure useful properties of surrounding water and to conduct basic bottom imagery). The other sensors indicate an offering based on user needs and requirements. It should be noted that the list in Table 9 is only aggressively advertised sensors from the UUV providers. It was evident during the research, that the UUV providers demonstrated many other sensors including ones unchecked in the table. A designer should consider what sensors are commercially available for UUV integration, how they typically interface with seawater and match that against requirements.

5. Launch & Recovery

All five UUVs analyzed launch and recover the UUVs on the surface. This should be a basic capability of all UUVs. In the next chapter, submerged UUV L&R, as an additionally capability, are discussed. Table 10 summarizes L&R methods for the five UUVs.

UUV System	L&R Basic CONOP	Very Close Proximity to Surface Craft	Recovery Process	Convincing in Open Ocean?
REMUS 600	L&R on Surface	Y	• Hook Lines By Hand Or Pole • Maneuver Under Crane • Vertical Lift From Water	N
HUGIN 1000	L&R on Surface	N	• Distant Line Capture • Maneuver To Tow • Winch Into Stern Ramp	Y
Explorer	L&R on Surface	Y	•Hook Lines By Hand Or Pole •Maneuver Under Crane •Vertical Lift From Water	N
Bluefin-12	L&R on Surface	Y	•Hook Lines By Hand Or Pole •Maneuver Under Crane •Vertical Lift From Water	N
Gavia Scientific	L&R on Surface	Y	• Small Close Proximity Boat • Two Man Manual Recovery	N

Table 10.   Summary of UUV Launch & Recovery Methods.

There was commonality with "simple" surface based launch and recovery techniques. The REMUS 600, Explorer and Bluefin-12 all utilize a close proximity "hooking" a line onto the UUV, maneuvering the ship and UUV into a favorable position, and then conducting a vertical lift. This technique was not a convincing open ocean rough water solution, but more suitable for fair weather operations. According to [33], the REMUS 600 upgraded the crane and developed a pole for the "hook" to mitigate the "hands on" factor, but still puts the primary operations ship very close to the UUV. The Gavia is unique to this group in the sense that it is small and can be lifted by two to three personnel, which eliminates the need for a crane, but requires personnel very close to the UUV and water.

The HUGIN 1000, and previously discussed REMUS 6000 (not summarized in Table 10), utilize a very similar technique that is effective in open ocean and does not depend on small boats, close maneuvering to the surfaced UUV, or men in/near the water.

The requirement for off-shore and all-weather, compared to fair weather and calm seas, is a vastly different range of needs and is a major consideration to the designer.

D.   CHAPTER SUMMARY

This chapter analyzed architectural attributes of the five selected UUV systems. Each vehicle system (REMUS, HUGIN, Explorer, Bluefin and Gavia) was studied individually with dedicated presentation and discussion of the following key architectural attributes:

1. Overall Vehicle Arrangement (Layout)
2. Form Factor, Propulsors & Control Surfaces
3. Energy System
4. Pressure Hulls and Wet Volume
5. Accommodations for Sensors
6. Communications
7. Launch & Recovery

After the attribute analysis of the UUVs a summary and discussion was presented based on the key architectural features. The summary and discussion was not meant to justify the UUV provider's logic when implementing certain architectural features, but to suggest key architecture considerations that a designer should consider. The UUVs selected have been successful in the marketplace and the discussion was aimed at presenting key considerations for designers/architects rather than assume decision justifications by the provider. Another UUV system, NAVOCEANO Seahorse, was introduced to support discussion of propulsors. The discussion of attributes was relevant to the UUVs presented, commonalities, trends and differences among them, not "generalized" as was the discussion of attributes in Chapter III. Certain relevant conclusions were made based on the summary, pros and cons of attribute considerations were presented where appropriate, and comments about the consideration to requirements were made throughout the summary.

V. RECOMMENDED UUV SYSTEM ARCHITECTURE ATTRIBUTES FOR THE NAVY

A. INTRODUCTION

This chapter is a discussion of recommended architectural attributes for notional UUV system planned for military use, more specifically for U.S. Navy use. The assumption is that these recommendations are for a proposed UUV system architecture *if* it were to be developed *now* based on analysis and discussions of the research in this thesis. The objective is to take "best of breed" from the UUV systems analyzed and incorporate into these notional recommended attributes. The focus of the seven groups of attributes analyzed and discussed in previous chapters is the theme and structure for recommendations summarized in this chapter.

The following best of breed architectural recommendations essentially addresses:

- <u>What</u> architectural attributes are recommended? There may be multiple recommendations based on assumptions of requirements or other drivers. The intent is to generalize attribute recommendations based on what was deemed "successful" in the marketplace, discussions of driving considerations and how a military application may factor into them.

- <u>Why</u> are they recommended (i.e., what is the basis)? This is an explanation of preferences of architectural attributes and a reasoning of their recommendation. The tenants of system engineering considerations and Navy application are major factors in addressing "why."

- Logical constraints or boundaries that would need to be considered if such attributes were actually integrated into Navy applications. Attributes of a system, existing or notional, will have constraints or boundaries that limit them.

- Potential impacts of military (Navy) application. A discussion of potential impacts to the recommended attributes and how Navy applications could influence modifications or other changes to them.

B. RECOMMENDED UUV ARCHITECTURAL ATTRIBUTES FOR MILITARY APPLICATION

1. Form factor, Control Surfaces and Propulsion

Recommended Form Factor: Torpedo-like with faired nose and afterbody.

The form factor of the selected UUVs analyzed, and most other UUVs researched, are all "torpedo-like" with a faired nose and afterbody, and a cylindrical main body. UUV providers have successfully incorporated a variety of pressure hulls, free-flood volumes, propulsors, sensors, hard-points and other handling provisions, and control surface schemes into torpedo-like form factors. The adage "if it's not broke don't fix it" applies here. There is also consideration for manufacturing and structural properties for both symmetry and cylinders. The manufacturing of symmetrical and cylindrical components is likely less expensive than compound complex curvature or asymmetric shapes. Symmetry is also more conducive to modularity. Structural properties and analysis of cylindrical and symmetric shapes is likely more predictable and less expensive.

The length-to-diameter ratio varied in UUV systems analyzed, but it is reasonable to assume there is a practical, efficient and hydrodynamically controllable limit to what the length-to-diameter ratio is. This would be a constraint to this recommendation. Another related constraint for consideration is the amount of "acceptable" lumps, bumps and other protrusions from the form-factor. All UUVs researched had exterior geometries (i.e., antennas, exposed sensors, handling equipment, etc.), which, if not controlled, could eventually drive excessive appendages and some smoother (faired) modifications to the symmetric torpedo shape may result (i.e., similar to a sail on a submarine). The low drag nature of the torpedo-like shape is degraded by appendages in the flow.

Naval applications favor a torpedo-like form factor. If the scale were appropriate and the form factor could be "smoothed" to 21 inches or less, a common Mk67 submarine torpedo tube could be utilized for launch and potentially for recovery. Other larger vertical tubes (i.e., missile boats or future Virginia class blocks) or submarine piggy-back structures (i.e., dry deck shelters) could be utilized. Torpedo-like form factors

100

would also be suitable for Naval surface ships which could be utilized similar to the way operation vessels support ocean going UUV operations now (see launch and recovery discussion in Chapter IV).

Recommended Control Surfaces: Far-aft control surfaces and optional forward control surfaces that are relatively "sheltered" from the vulnerabilities of snagging, fouling and breakage.

To implement a rugged and robust UUV in military applications would likely involve operations near shore, in fishing areas or other areas with some degree of water column clutter or debris (intentional or unintentional). "Soft" debris or obstacles in the form of ropes, lines, nylon string, kelp, etc…may not be visible to a UUV's obstacle avoidance capability (if the UUV even has it). This assumption drives the desire to minimize susceptibility to line-type snags, snares, etc. The Gavia vehicle (see Figure 84) successfully implemented control surfaces that are embedded in the propulsor shroud. The shroud and its fixed support vanes may help divert line (and other) debris away from the propeller and the controls surfaces. This design is certainly considered less vulnerable than other UUV systems with very "proud" control surfaces exposed to the flow near the vehicle. The NAVOCEANO Seahorse (see Figure 89) also has a control surface design that will discourage fouling or entanglement. The control surfaces on the Seahorse are also "far aft" and their leading edges are protected by the shroud/propulsor design.

Chapter IV also discussed the benefit of the control surfaces being located just aft of the propeller (or rotor) to add lifting efficiency to the fins by being in accelerated flow. This is another reason the "far-aft" (i.e., in the propeller wake) control surfaces are recommended.

Different UUV systems investigated have forward control surfaces, see Figures 56, 74 and 77 as examples. This option is also very appealing. UUVs operating at very slow speeds, with several potential factors contributing to difficulty of hydrodynamic control, are likely to have the need for more fin authority. Such driving factors in Naval applications are possibly operations in a shallow surf zone or a sensor or payload that

101

challenges the controllability of the vehicle. Obviously, forward fins are also recommended to be "sheltered" or somehow protected from entanglement. This is discussed further later in this chapter.

Recommended Propulsor: Ducted (or shrouded) propeller.

A shrouded propeller (or rotor) is desirable for a few key reasons. First, indications are (see propulsor discussion in Chapter IV) that ducted or shrouded propulsors offer more efficiency in water. Second, there is clearly a safety benefit associated with a "covered" blade row that spins, especially during launch, recovery and handling operations. The last driver for this recommendation is indicated in the previous section; the shroud may help divert entanglement to both the blade-row and the control surfaces (depending on their location).

For Navy application, a shrouded propulsor is viewed more beneficial based on three major reasons above. These three arguments for a shrouded propulsor are not viewed as unique to Navy or military applications and have been used successfully in commercial applications.

2. Energy

Recommended Energy Source: Certified pressure tolerant lithium rechargeable battery (possibly in standard modules).

The discussion in Chapter III points to rechargeable (secondary) lithium (ion or polymer) batteries as an obvious choice for UUV energy. The analysis of UUVs showed lithium batteries *are* the obvious choice (see Table 7) for commercial applications. The recommendation for Navy applications is based on this investigation and the successful UUVs utilizing lithium ion or polymer in the commercial marketplace.

One issue discussed throughout the research material is the safety concern with an energy dense battery such as lithium-ion or lithium-polymer. The Bluefin Robotics Inc. pressure tolerant battery underwent rigorous (abusive) tests per a specification from the Naval Sea Systems Command (NAVSEA) referred to as Instruction 9310.1b which specifies the lithium battery certification process for the U.S. submarine force. According to [46], at completion of the testing, the Bluefin battery was approved for Navy use (shipping, handling and surface ship operations). Kongsberg's HUGIN, which also uses pressure tolerant lithium batteries, sought and received United Nation (UN) approval to transport HUGIN batteries as hazardous material [9]. This is why a "certified" pressure tolerant lithium battery is recommended. The certification for shipping, handling, storing and operating (includes recharging) is a *must* for Naval application. The Bluefin batteries boast this accomplishment for surface ship based operations with one particular battery configuration, but not submarine use. The lithium battery recommended would be required to undergo further certification process (i.e., submarine safety program requirements) in order to be utilized onboard a submarine.

The choice of a pressure tolerant battery is based on two basic reasons. First, the HUGIN and Bluefin open-source information did a convincing job of justifying "why" they use pressure tolerant batteries. They argue points like the elimination of costly and heavy pressure hulls, more conducive to deeper diving UUVs, along with other safety and heat-transfer related benefits. The second reason to prefer the pressure tolerant battery is related to preference of free-flood vehicle architecture (discussed later).

The last recommendation related to UUV energy is; the Navy should consider developing (i.e., conduct a study) a standard lithium battery, built in modules that can be certified for mobilization, use and recharging as a stand-alone system. This offers a big benefit to the Navy to have an open architecture modular energy system that could be utilized by multiple UUV providers for multiple mission requirements and systems. Four of the UUV systems analyzed had similar system voltages ranging from 30V to 50V (the fifth (Gavia) UUV battery voltage was unknown). Admittedly, the exact loading and power rates demanded of these batteries by the UUV is unknown, but preliminary indications (in this study) are the UUV power demands and bus voltage designs are similar and a common battery module is feasible.

3. Pressure Hulls and Wet Volume

Recommended Hull/Volume Philosophy: Free-flood dominates.

The UUVs selected for the architectural attribute analysis, were selected in part for the varying preferences for dry pressure volumes versus wet (free-flood) volumes. This enabled systems discussion of both. As discussed in Chapter III and Chapter IV, most UUV's incorporate both philosophies in their architecture to some degree, but in general, a UUV provider leans toward a dominant philosophy in the system design of pressure vessels or free-flood. The discussion about hull volume preference included many pros and cons with each method. The recommendation is for a dominate free-flood design philosophy.

The primary basis for this recommendation is *the sensors and batteries*. The UUVs both researched and analyzed had a substantial amount of sensors (i.e., communication and navigation transducers, imaging sonar's, CTD's, other oceanographic measuring devices, altimeters, tracking equipment, emergency pingers, cameras, etc.) that were all designed for and in free-flood sections. As discussed earlier, UUV providers that utilize pressure tolerant batteries (i.e., in the free-flood) argued convincingly the benefits to these types of batteries and the batteries are a substantial volumetric component to the overall UUV. It was shown in Chapter IV that free-flood vehicles with dry batteries (i.e., ISE Explorer and Boeing Echo Ranger) simply have a larger pressure vessel to accommodate the batteries. The recommended design would have to accommodate dry components, which is unavoidable, but with wet pressure tolerant batteries, the dry volumes would be minimized. The HUGIN dedicates two spheres for dry equipment: hotel and payload, which best represents the approach recommended here.

The secondary basis for this recommendation is the conduciveness to deeper depth capability. Chapter III and Chapter IV discussions indicated that free-flood dominant systems are more likely as depth capability increases. This is preferred for a system in the Navy that may have a wide degree of depth requirements. Free-flood architecture would be a less risky and less expensive transition to a "deep requirement."

4.   Sensors and Communications

Recommended Sensors: A baseline suite (see below) and others as needed.

Sensors on a UUV are very mission specific and for the most part would (and should) be driven by requirements. For example, a UUV mission that is conducting ocean floor reconnaissance would have sensors geared towards "downward looking" imagery, possibly consisting of sub-bottom profilers, magnetometers, side scan sonars, synthetic aperture sonars, cameras, etc. A mission for surface data collection would have sensors geared for signal intercept on an antenna/mast assembly. The sensors selected are primarily mission dependent.

When analyzing the five UUV systems, however, certain sensors were "common" to all UUV systems and were considered "baseline" as a result. Recall that Table 9 summarized sensors and communications hardware on the UUVs studied. Sensor that were not specific to communications or navigation that are considered the "baseline suite" are:

- Side Scan Sonar
- Conductivity, Temperature and Density
- Cameras

These baseline sensors were typical to the five successful and diverse UUV systems in the marketplace and are considered as coming "standard" with a UUV system for the Navy. They provide a basic ability for bottom imagery, video/stills in directions of interest and important water properties (defining the acoustic environment). Consistent with the free-flood dominant discussion earlier, these three standard sensors are assumed to reside in the free flood.

There are also several UUV sensors that are dedicated to navigation and typical UUV vehicle (housekeeping) operations that were not the focused on in this analysis. Analyzing these types (i.e., vehicle and navigation based) of sensors was not in the scope of this study. These sensors typically include: Acoustic Doppler Current Profiler (navigation aid that was discussed), depth sensors, altimeters, leak sensors, temperature sensors, electrical current sensors, voltage sensors, etc. A higher end UUV with aided inertial navigation, casualty monitoring systems, autopilot, flight control, etc. was assumed for a UUV recommended to the Navy, which would include these types of sensors.

The integration of sensors was reviewed and discussed in Chapter III and Chapter IV. Most sensors needed exposure to the water column and an unobstructed view outward. The side-scan sonar and cameras are examples of this, which would be a condition for these systems integration. The CTD needs to "grab" seawater, but only requires a port (i.e., plumbing) in the hull to do so.

Recommended Communications: RF Wi-Fi, Iridium SATCOM, 2-Way Acoustic Telemetry and GPS Receive.

The communication gear implemented into commercial UUV systems was common across the board for the UUVs analyzed (refer to Table 9). These communication capabilities were clearly a common suite for UUV communications and are a straight forward recommendation to the Navy. The Wi-Fi RF Ethernet is a short range communication system used at-sea, on-deck and "in the shop" for these UUV systems. The Iridium satellite communication system is a low data rate near global communication method. The acoustic communications was also a common capability, but through the medium of water and not air. Some tracking and emergency location equipment is 1-way communications…the intent here for Navy use is 2-way acoustic communications. Finally, all UUVs investigated utilize GPS geo-location signals for navigation.

The RF, Iridium and GPS antennas all typically reside on top of the UUV with some means of elevation off the surface of the water (i.e., a mast). The acoustic communication transducers varied in location on the vehicle. Systems with typical deep dive operations (i.e., HUGIN) have the acoustic communications transducers on top of the UUV or "upward looking," systems with more shallow applications typically have the transducers on the bottom of the UUV to ensure functionality when the UUV is at or near the surface.

The missing component to UUV communication for Navy applications is the military aspect to communication and control of war fighting assets. Other methods of communications are available for UUV military communications (i.e., UHF SATCOM), but are not part of this discussion. Suffice it to say a Navy UUV system should include

106

the latest and most common commercially available systems for development, industry related and academic type endeavors. Other communication methods and equipment could be used as needed per requirements of the Navy.

5. Launch and Recovery

<u>Recommended L&R</u>: Surfaced UUV Stern Ramp / Gun Grapple Recovery Line and Submerged Whisker UUV Line Capture

The recommended launch and recovery technique is a two-fold recommendation. The first is the recovery method utilized by both the REMUS 6000 (shown in Figure 62) and the HUGIN 1000 (shown in Figures 70 and 71). The technique consists of a pivoting (motion compensating) stern ramp on an ocean-going surface ship, relatively long range grappling a recovery line that has deployed from the UUV nose, and a winched recovery while the UUV is in tow. Figure 70 shows the sequence well and Figures 62 and 71 show the stern ramps clearly. The technique is proven in open-ocean operations with the UUV deployed and recovered from the surface. The stern ramp has been shown (both by Kongsberg and Hydroid) to fit multiple ship configurations utilizing "typical" power and hydraulics. It is assumed such accommodations can be provided on a Navy surface ship (i.e., Littoral Combatant Ship, MCM class or others).

The second recommendation requires brief discussion of UUV launch and recovery techniques that are *not* typical to the commercial sector. First to discuss is the Lockheed Martin Marlin UUV (Figure 50) which utilizes a submerged launch and recovery method from vertical cable in the water column. According to [23] and [24], the UUV can release-and-launch or capture-and-recover utilizing an acoustic homing system and a "whisker" line capture/release mechanism. Figure 91 shows the Marlin approaching the cable and secured at the top of the recovery cable.

Approaching Recovery Cable | Maneuvering Up the Cable After Capture

Figure 91.   Lockheed Martin Marlin Approaching Recovery Cable and Maneuvering
Up Cable After Capture, after [24].

On approach, the whiskers straddle the cable and guide it into the locking latch, once locked in (i.e., captured) the UUV can maneuver with thrusters or changes in buoyancy up or down the cable.

The second method to discuss is the Hydroid REMUS 100 submerged docking station. According to [57], the REMUS homes acoustically on a transponder and the UUV swims (with some guidance from a funnel shaped entrance) into the stationary cage. Figure 92 shows the REMUS 100 in the launch and recovery station.

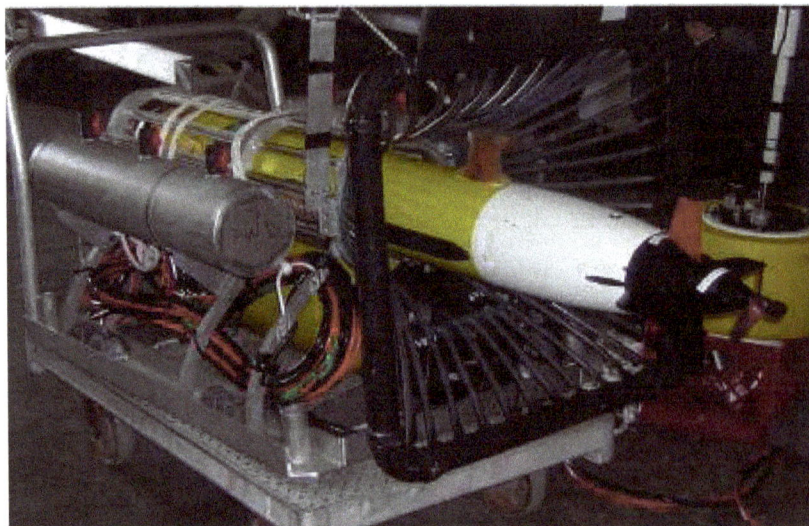

Figure 92.   Hydroid REMUS 100 in Docking Station, from [57].

After the REMUS enters the cage, alignment pins and connections are made to provide power and communications to the UUV [57].

The second recommended launch and recovery method for Navy application is the whisker UUV line capture similar to the Marlin system. The system has been developed and demonstrated to add credibility to the method. The line capture is the preferred "piece" of the L&R system. A vertical cable could be suspended *down* from a surface ship or *up* from a submarine or bottom station and offers some flexibility of platform. The captured UUV could be pulled to a platform or a hole with the aid of the UUV itself. Navy applications for UUVs are likely not always inclusive of surface ships. This rationale is what drives a second L&R option in addition to the more "commercial" surface ship recovery (first recommendation). This method puts options in potential deploy and recovery CONOP of a submerged UUV.

C.   CHAPTER SUMMARY

This chapter presents and discusses recommended architectural attributes for a UUV that would notionally be acquired and operated by the Navy. The previous chapters in this thesis frame the nature of the recommendations and kept the design suggestions "in-line" with key attributes that have been focused on. The attribute recommendations were structured to address what, why, significant constraints, and application in the Navy.

The key architectural attribute not discussed thus far is the layout recommended for this UUV. As discussed in Chapter III, the layout tends to be the resultant of decisions with regards to systems architecture with the influence of "packaging." This is why the layout is discussed here in the chapter summary after the other key attributes were already discussed.

Figure 93 shows a notional external layout that includes some of the key recommendations to UUV system architecture presented. This sketch shows what the notional Navy UUV may look like based on the recommendations and discussions in this chapter.

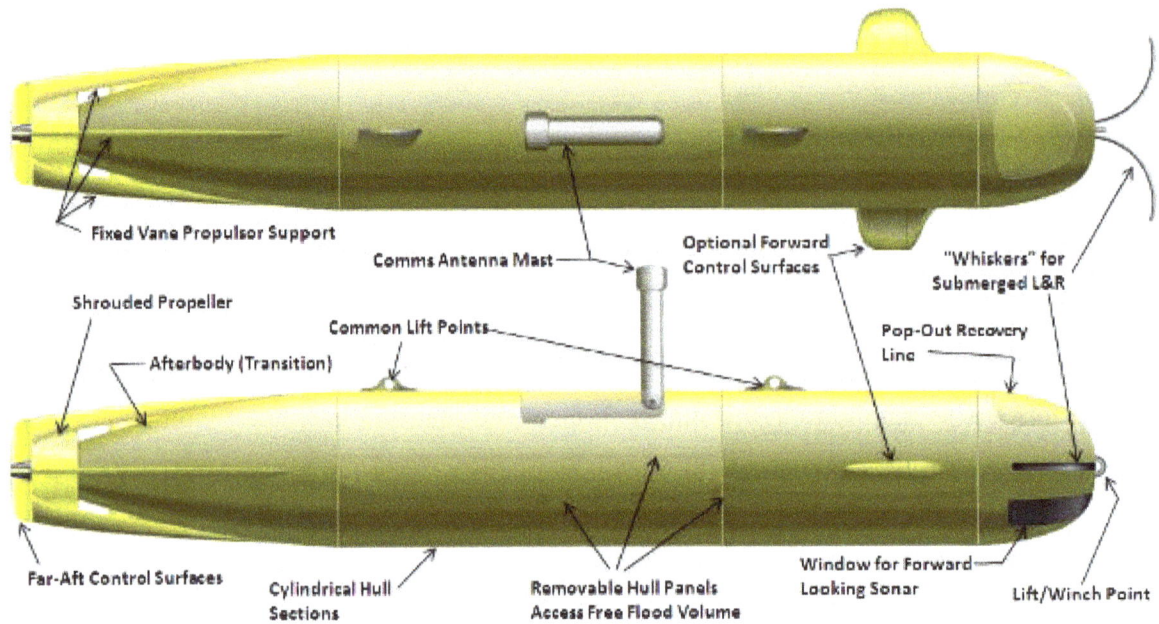

Figure 93.   Notional Navy UUV Form Factor and Architectural Attributes Based on Analysis Results and Preferences. The top graphic is the top view of the UUV and the bottom graphic is the side view.

The following attributes were incorporated into the concept drawing in Figure 93:

The form factor is torpedo-like with faired nose and afterbody. The figure shows the torpedo-like shape, cylinder based with a smooth transition from nose to parallel mid-body and from mid-body to tail. The afterbody transitions flow from the mid-body into the propulsor inlet.

Far-aft control surfaces and optional forward control surfaces that are relatively "sheltered" from the vulnerabilities of snagging, fouling and breakage are integrated into this notional design. The aft control surfaces are immediately aft of the shrouded propeller where their leading edges are protected by the fixed vanes or contained within the diameter of the shroud. The optional forward control surfaces have the leading edge both curved and fixed to encourage soft debris "flow off" the fin and discourage entanglement.

The propulsor is a ducted (or shrouded) propeller. The propeller is not shown, but proposed to be within the shroud's inner diameter. The inlet to the propeller is formed by

110

the aft end of the afterbody. The flow of water would proceed through the propeller, over the exposed portion of the "+" configuration control surfaces and into the UUV's wake.

The energy section (not shown) is envisioned to be a certified pressure tolerant lithium rechargeable battery located inside the hull sections. The location is likely within the cylindrical hull form since the batteries are large components.

The hull inner volume proposed (not shown) is "free-flood" dominant. The design would accommodate a free-flooded component layout arrangement. Seams are shown, representative of panels or sections of hull form that would be integral to the UUV's free-flood philosophy.

The baseline suite of sensors includes:
- Side Scan Sonar
- Conductivity, Temperature and Density (CTD) Sensor
- Cameras

These sensors are not shown in the figure, but, as discussed earlier, the side scan sonar would be flush with the hull with direct exposure to seawater with a line-of-sight in the desired orientation. The CTD sensor would reside within the free-flooded sections with appropriate plumbing to the sensing component. The cameras would also be configured to suitable orientation in the free-flood, similar to the sonar.

The baseline airborne communications suite would include integrating the RF Wi-Fi antenna, Iridium SATCOM antenna and GPS receive antenna into the communications antenna mast which is shown in Figure 93. The mast is proposed as "fold down" to remain consistent with the low vulnerability to entanglement philosophy while underway (i.e., submerged swimming). The mechanics of the mast's deploy and retract concept are not addressed other than including a pivot feature and a pocket volume for stowage. The 2-way acoustic telemetry transducers (not shown) would reside in the free-flood with direct exposure to seawater and desired orientation on the hull.

The notional UUV in Figure 93 incorporates indicators of the desired launch and recovery (L&R) method: UUV stern ramp / gun grapple recovery line and submerged whisker UUV line capture. The nose of the UUV shows a lift/hoist point (i.e., a pad-eye) to accommodate line retrieval (nose haul) into a stern ramp. Notional whiskers are shown (both retracted and extended) to represent the capability for submerged line-capture. The top of the UUV has lift points to accommodate "normal" lifting from the surface or during regular handling operations in air. The nose section also accommodates a hatch where the recovery line would deploy.

The last notable attribute, the nose section also shows a notional forward look sonar (below the whiskers) to indicate a likely use of remaining "forward looking" real estate on the vehicle.

This notional layout, while only a sketch, is a representative layout and form factor of the recommended system architecture for Navy applications.

VI. SUMMARY AND CONCLUSIONS

A. SUMMARY

This thesis conducted a broad open-source survey of existing unmanned undersea vehicles (UUVs) that are present in the market place today. Five UUV systems were determined to be prominent in the market place; meaning they had significant sales (i.e., success) and established manufacturing capability. These five systems were:

1. Hydroid REMUS 600
2. Kongsberg HUGIN 1000
3. ISE Explorer
4. Bluefin Robotic Inc's Bluefin-12
5. Gavia Scientific

Other UUV systems were introduced to augment discussion of particular architectural features including: Lockheed Martin Marlin, Boeing Echo Ranger, NAVOCEANO Seahorse, REMUS 6000 and REMUS 100.

Key architectural attributes for UUV systems are defined and discussed. The discussion involved primary considerations a system architect should address when developing a UUV system. Attribute benefits (pros) and detriments (cons) were studied as well as associated constraints and boundaries a designer must contemplate. These considerations included drivers (i.e., environment, requirements) and other influencing factors that may persuade the final product. The seven key attributes were all in the context of UUV architecture and listed below:

1. Overall Vehicle Arrangement (Layout)
2. Form Factor, Propulsors & Control Surfaces
3. Energy System
4. Pressure Hulls and Wet Volume
5. Accommodations for Sensors
6. Communications
7. Launch & Recovery

An analysis was conducted with a comprehensive presentation of each key architectural attributes on each of the five selected UUV systems. This analysis is summarized and a comparison of the results is presented. Commonalities, trends, and differences were presented as part of the comparison. The analysis summary included further conclusive discussion of system architectural considerations that a designer/architect should be considering in the design, development, and operations of UUV systems.

Finally, recommendations are made regarding what architectural attributes would be recommended for a new UUV introduced into the U.S. Navy for operational use. The recommendations were structured in-line with the key attributes presented and analyzed in earlier chapters. The recommendations consisted of defining "what" they were, "why" they were recommended and "how" they could be applied and impacted by Navy use. These recommendations were partially incorporated into a notional UUV external layout/form factor (Figure 93) to help facilitate and visualize the architectural attributes suggested.

B. KEY POINTS AND RECOMMENDATIONS

It was determined that analyzing UUV system architecture in established commercial UUV systems would lead to an educated insight into these systems, greater insight into UUV architecture in general, and a basis from which to recommend application into Navy use.

A survey was conducted, looking at open-source information on commercial UUV systems. The survey consisted of thirty-four (34) different UUV systems being offered by UUV providers (industry). Main capabilities and characteristics of these UUV were provided in the survey.

Five UUV systems were determined "prominent" in the marketplace, delivered in a "turn-key" manner, and having sufficient open source material to support analysis. Prominent in the marketplace is considered to be UUVs sold in significant enough numbers to be considered "high production," where a repeatable manufacturing of one system architecture is apparently established by the provider. The "turn-key" delivery indicates the provider sells the UUV system and field equipment so the buyer is encouraged to independently operate it. Some UUV providers did not appear to have mature deployment and operational products, and gave a "feel" that they (the provider) wanted to stay connected to the UUV operations of the client. The open source material availability for learning, analysis, and discussion is self-explanatory.

Other UUV systems, considered "low production," are introduced throughout the thesis to help reinforce discussion about particular architectural attributes. Examples are the Hydroid REMUS 6000, Hydroid REMUS 100, NAVOCEANO Seahorse, Boeing Echo Ranger and Lockheed Martin Marlin.

Key UUV architectural attributes are selected and discussed from a systems engineering perspective. The attributes are discussed in context to UUV operations and to key considerations a designer/architect must make in UUV system development. The considerations are introduced in Chapter III and discussions included drivers, requirements, engineering trade-studies, and other influences for the architect's consideration.

Each selected "high production" UUV system is analyzed relative to each key architectural attribute. The UUV systems and their architectural attributes are comprehensively presented in Chapter IV. The presentation included an explanation of each system/attribute combination and discussed considerations the system architect and engineers likely considered before implementing into their systems. The discussions were not aimed at understanding exactly "why" *every* decision was made by the UUV providers, but to understand (in general) likely factors that drove the product's architecture.

A comparison of UUV system attributes was then conducted (Chapter IV) which looked at commonalities, differences and trends amongst the UUV systems attributes. The comparison discussion includes potential considerations for the architects and how established and proven the attributes were. This comparison discussion includes a table summary of each UUV system and preferences for the architectural attributes.

In a conclusive discussion, Chapter V offers recommendations for a notional Navy UUV system based on discussions and points in preceding chapters. The recommendations are made based on preferences and inclinations formed throughout the thesis. The recommendations explained "what" was recommended, "why" the recommended attributes were suggested (i.e., reasons, justifications), and "how" these recommendations are applicable (and potentially impacted) to Navy applications. These recommendations are summarized below:

- Recommended Form Factor: Torpedo-like with faired nose and afterbody.

- Recommended Control Surfaces: Far-aft control surfaces and optional forward control surfaces that are relatively "sheltered" from the vulnerabilities of snagging, fouling and breakage.

- Recommended Propulsor: Ducted (or shrouded) propeller.

- Recommended Energy Source: Certified pressure tolerant lithium rechargeable battery (possibly in standard modules).

- Additional recommendation related to UUV energy; the Navy should consider developing (i.e., conduct a study) a standard lithium battery, built in modules that can be certified for mobilization, use and recharging as a stand-alone system.

- Recommended Hull/Volume Philosophy: Free-flood dominant.

- Recommended Sensors: A baseline suite (see below) and others as needed.

- Side Scan Sonar

- Conductivity, Temperature and Density

- Cameras

- Recommended Communications: RF Wi-Fi, Iridium SATCOM, 2-Way Acoustic Telemetry and GPS Receive.

- Recommended L&R: Surfaced UUV Stern Ramp / Gun Grapple Recovery Line and Submerged Whisker UUV Line Capture

C.   AREAS TO CONDUCT FURTHER RESEARCH

One area for further research would be to increase the amount of UUV systems surveyed and analyzed to include systems developed by academia, Navy laboratories, and systems unique to military applications. These systems were not in the scope of this thesis, as there was a focus on commercially established and successful UUV systems.

Another potential path to further research is to address open-ocean UUV gliders. Gliders were not included in the scope of this thesis, and offer a unique UUV system architecture to analyze, break down features, and make recommendations for Navy operations. Gliders appear to have significant market presence where a similar thesis/study could be conducted on this unique UUV platform.

Another way to expand this thesis into further research would be to simply select more (new) architectural attributes to select, analyze and to recommend for Naval applications. Other important UUV architecture attributes include navigation methods (i.e., state of the art, in GPS denied areas, etc.), internal processing hardware, information handling and software (i.e., open vs closed architectures, information assurance methods, etc.), autonomous adaptive controllers, advanced energy sources and reliability.

To map architectural characteristics with existing and potential UUV mission areas is another potential area for further research that would allow attribute evaluation in its proper context.

Finally, research into U.S Navy UUV lifecycle considerations such as logistics, supportability, training, etc, is likely a needed area for further study as well.

THIS PAGE INTENTIONALLY LEFT BLANK

LIST OF REFERENCES

[1]   Autonomous Undersea Vehicles Applications Center, Lee, NH, AUVAC Web site [Online], Available: http://www.auvac.org. [Accessed: May 2010].

[2]   Department of the Navy, "The Navy Unmanned Undersea Vehicle (UUV) Master Plan," U.S. Navy Web site, November 2004   [Online], Available: https//www.navy.mil [Accessed: December 2004].

[3]   Admiral Vern Clark, "Sea Power 21, Projecting Decisive Joint Capabilities," U.S. Navy, Proceedings, October 2002.

[4]   Hydroid LLC, Pocasset, MA, Hydroid Web site [Online], Available: http://www.hydroid.com [Accessed: June 2010].

[5]   R. W. Button, J. Kamp, T. B. Curtin, J. Dryden, "A survey of missions for unmanned undersea vehicles," RAND National Defense Research Institute Web site, 2009 [Online], Available: www.rand.org [Accessed: May 10, 2010].

[6]   Hydroid, LLC, Pocasset, MA, "REMUS 600 Autonomous Underwater Vehicle (brochure)," Hydroid Web site [Online], Available: http://www.hydroid.com./pdfs/remus600web.pdf [Accessed May 11, 2010].

[7]   Hydroid, LLC, Pocasset, MA, "REMUS 6000 Autonomous Underwater Vehicle," product brochure, Hydroid Web site [Online], Available: http://www.hydroid.com/pdfs/remus6000web.pdf [Accessed May 11, 2010].

[8]   Kongsberg Maritime, Kongsberg, Norway, Kongsberg Maritime Web site Online], Available: http://www.km.kongsberg.com [Accessed: May 2010].

[9]   Kongsberg Maritime, Kongsberg, Norway, "Autonomous Underwater Vehicle – AUV, The HUGIN Family," product brochure, Kongsberg Maritime Web site [Online], Available: http://www.km.kongsberg.com/ks/web/nokbg0397.nsf/AllWeb/A6A2CC361D3B 9653C1256D71003E97D5/$file/HUGIN_Family_brochure_r2_lr.pdf [Accessed July 19, 2010].

[10]   E. Hagen, N. Storkersen, B. Marthinsen, G. Sten, K. Vestgard, "Rapid environmental assessment with autonomous underwater vehicles – Examples from HUGIN operations" Journal of Maritime Systems, vol. 69, pp. 137–145, 2008.

[11]   International Submarine Engineering Limited, Port Coquitlam, BC, Canada, ISE Web site [Online], Available: http://www.ise.bc.ca [Accessed: May 2010].

[12] International Submarine Engineering Limited, Port Coquitlam, BC, Canada, "Corporate profile," ISE Web site, February 23, 2010. [Online], Available: http://www.ise.bc.ca/AboutUs/ISE%20Corporate%20Profile%202008.pdf [Accessed May 11, 2010].

[13] International Submarine Engineering Limited, Port Coquitlam, BC, Canada, "ISE Receives New Contract to Build AUVs," ISE Web site, ISE press release, November 13, 2008 [Online], Available: http://www.ise.bc.ca/AboutUs/ISE-E172-BRC-001-01.pdf [Accessed May 11, 2010].

[14] University of Bremen, Marum Center for Marine Environmental Sciences, Bremen, Marum Web site [Online], Available:http://www.marum.de/en/Picture_Gallery.html [Accessed: June 2010].

[15] Bluefin Robotics Corporation, Cambridge, MA, Bluefin Web site [Online], Available: http://www.bluefinrobotics.com [Accessed: June 2010]

[16] B. Abraham, J. Bales, "Bluefin's AUVs: Current and Potential Low-Observability Missions," Ocean News & Technology, Palm City, vol. 12, iss. 6, p. 34, November/December 2006.

[17] A. Steingrimsson, H. Ehf, A. McMurtrie, "The Great Northern Diver," GAVIA Autonomous Undersea Vehicles Web site, International Ocean Systems, June 2010 [Online], Available: http://www.gavia.is/resources/Files/6-Media-Coverage/2010 06 Int.Ocean Systems CoverStory.pdf [Accessed June 13, 2010].

[18] Hafmynd ehf, Kopavogur, Iceland, GAVIA Autonomous Undersea Vehicles Web site [Online], Available: http://www.gavia.is [Accessed: June 2010]

[19] Hafmynd ehf, Kopavogur, Iceland, "GAVIA – The Great Northern Diver," Roper Resources Web site, GAVIA brochure [Online], Available: http://www.roperresources.com/pdfs/GaviaBrochure0402.pdf [Accessed June 10, 2010].

[20] M. Merrill, "Existing Operational Unmanned Systems as Mobile Networked Nodes," Marine Technology Journal, December 2007.

[21] Anonymous , "Lockheed Martin Introduces Marlin (TM)," , Ocean News & Technology, 15, 8; Research Library, p. 36, December 2009.

[22] Lockheed Martin Corporation, Arlington., VA, Lockheed Martin Web site [Online], Available: http://www.lockheedmartin.com [Accessed: June 2010].

[23] Anonymous, "Lockheed Martin: Taking AUV Technology to the Next Level," Ocean News & Technology, Palm City, vol. 16, iss. 3, p. 42, April 2010.

[24] Lockheed Martin, Maritime System and Sensors, Washington, DC, "Lockheed Martin Marlin Autonomous Underwater Vehicle," Lockheed Martin Web site, product brochure [Online], Available: http://www.lockheedmartin.com/data/assets/ms2/pdf/MARLIN.pdf [Accessed June 9, 2010].

[25] E. Dzielski, C. Tangirala, W. W. Moyer, D.L. Bradley, "NAVOCEANO Seahorse AUV design, testing, and capabilities," OCEANS '02 MTS/IEEE, vol. 1, Digital Object Identifier; 10.1109/OCEANS.2002.1193263, vol 1, pp. 151–155, 2002.

[26] S. Tangirala, J. Dzielski, "A variable buoyancy control system for a large AUV," Oceanic Engineering, IEEE Journal of, vol. 32, iss. 4, Digital Object Identifier: 10.1109/JOE.2007.911596, pp. 762–771, 2007.

[27] S. A. Sharkh, D. Doerffel, "Large Lithium-Ion Batteries – a Review," REAPsystems, Ltd. Web site, October 14 [Online], Available: http://reapsystems.co.uk/_publications/EMA2006final.pdf [Accessed June 11, 2010].

[28] V. Srinivasan, "Batteries for Vehicular Applications," Lawrence Berkeley National Lab, Berkeley, CA Web site, September 2008 [Online], Available: http://berc.lbl.gov/venkat/files/batteries-for-vehicles.pdf [Accessed June 11, 2010].

[29] D. Linden and T. B. Reddy, Handbook of Batteries, 3rd Ed., McGraw-Hill, Inc., 2002.

[30] R. P. Stokey, C. von Alt, B. Allen, N. Forrester, T. Austin, R. Goldsborough, M. Purcell, F. Jaffre, G. Packard, A. Kukulya, A. Roup, "Development of the REMUS 600 Autonomous Underwater Vehicle," IEEE Oceans 2005 Conference proceedings, Woods Hole Oceanographic Institution and Vehicle Control Technology.

[31] Woods Hole Oceanographic Institution, Woods Hole, MA, WHOI Web site [Online], Available: http://www.whoi.edu.

[32] NUWC REMUS 600 Photos, Naval Undersea Warfare Center Division Newport, AUV Division, Newport, RI, July 16, 2010.

[33] C. G. Rauch, M.J. Purcell, T. Austin, G.J. Packard, "Ship of opportunity launch and recovery system for REMUS 600 AUV's," OCEANS 2008 IEEE Conferences, Digital Object Identifier: 10.1109/OCEANS.2008.5151832, pp. 1–4, 2008.

[34] C. von Alt, B. Allen, T. Austin, N. Forrester, L. Freitag, R. Goldsborough, M. Grund, M. Purcell, R. Stokey, "Semiautonomous mapping systems," OCEANS 2003 IEEE Conferences proceedings, vol. 3, pp. 1709–1717, 2003.

[35]   M. Whitford, "In the Swim," GPS World, 16(4), 14–16, 18, 20, 22. Retrieved July 14, 2010, from ProQuest Science Journals. (Document ID: 824058121), (April 2005).

[36]   O. Hasvold, N. J. Storkersen, S. Forseth, T. Lian, "Power sources for autonomous underwater vehicles," Journal of Power Sources, vol. 162, pp. 935–942, 2006.

[37]   J. Ferguson, "Using AUVs in under-ice scientific missions, International Submarine Engineering Ltd., Presented at Arctic Change 08, Quebec City, Canada, December 11, 2008.

[38]   National Oceanic and Atmospheric Administration's Undersea Research Center & University of North Carolina – Wilmington, "NURC/SEGM Capabilities: Deepwater AUV," University of North Carolina Wilmington Web site [Online], Available: http://www.uncw.edu/nurc/auv/docs/auv one pager.pdf [Accessed May 11, 2010].

[39]   International Submarine Engineering, Ltd., Port Coquitlam, BC, Canada, "Explorer Autonomous Underwater Vehicle (AUV)," ISE Web site [Online], Available: http://www.ise.bc.ca/pdfs/Explorer%202009 2.pdf [Accessed May 4, 2010].

[40]   J. Ferguson, "Under-ice seabed mapping with AUVs," OCEANS 2009-EUROPE, 2009. OCEANS '09, Digital Object identifier: 10.1109/OCEANS.2009.5278204, pp. 1–6, 2009.

[41]   J. Ferguson, A. Pope, "Explorer-a modular AUV for commercial site survey," Underwater Technology, UT 00, Proceedings of the 2000 International Symposium on, Digital Object Identifier: 10.1109/UT.2000.852528, pp. 129–132, 2000.

[42]   G. Sulzbergera, J. Bonoa, G. L. Allena, T. Clem, and S. Kumar, "Demonstration of the real-time tracking gradiometer for buried mine hunting while operating from a small unmanned underwater vehicle," OCEANS 2006, Digital Object Identifier: 10.1109/OCEANS.2006.307094, pp. 1–5, 2006.

[43]   S. Willcox, J. Bondaryk, K. Streitlien, C. Emblen, and J. Morrison, "A Bluefin-12 based system solution for the US Navy's surface mine counter-measures unmanned underwater vehicle program: increment 2 (SMCM/UUV-2)," Bluefin Robotics Corporation Web site, May 3, 2007 [Online], Available: http://www.bluefinrobotics.com/PR2007/Bluefin12BasedUUVSystemforSMCM UUV203MAY07.pdf [Accessed May 25, 2010].

122

[44] R. LeBouvier, "Addressing priority needs with AUV technology," Underwater Unexploded Ordnance Workshop October 2008, CEROS National Defense Center of Excellence for Research in Ocean Sciences Web site [Online], Available: http://www.ceros.org/resources/briefings.htm [Accessed July 21, 2010].

[45] R. Panish, "Dynamic Control Capabilities and Developments of the Bluefin Robotics AUV Fleet," Bluefin Robotics Corporation, Cambridge, MA, UUST, July 2009.

[46] K. E. Robinson, "Li-poly pressure-tolerant batteries dive deep," Bluefin Robotics Corp., Battery Power Products & Technology, vol. 11, iss. 2, March/April 2007.

[47] "Vehicles – Untethered vehicles – Man-portable AUVs," United States; Bluefin-12, Jane's, February 16, 2010.

[48] R. Yeo, "Surveying the underside of an arctic ice ridge using a man-portable GAVIA AUV deployed through the ice," OCEANS 2007 IEEE Conferences, Digital Object Identifier: 10.1109/OCEANS.2007.4449402, pp. 1–8, 2007.

[49] University of California, Tahoe Environmental Research Center, Lake Tahoe, CA, "GAVIA AUV Pictures," UC Davis Tahoe Environmental Research Center Web site [Online], Available: http://www.terc.ucdavis.edu [Accessed: June 2010]

[50] Hafmynd ehf, Iceland, "GAVIA Scientific, GAVIA Autonomous Underwater Vehicle," GAVIA Autonomous Undersea Vehicles Web site, product brochure [Online], Available: http://www.gavia.is/resources/Files/Data-download/Product-Handouts-(Low-Res)/GaviaAUV_Scientific_lowres.pdf [Accessed June 10, 2010].

[51] Hydro Products, Ltd., Scotland, UK, "GAVIA Special Battery Module," Hydro-products Web site [Online], Available: http://www.hydro-products.co.uk [Accessed: June 2010]

[52] R. Mueller, "Compact GAVIA AUV proves inspection capability during Australia trials," ProQuest Science Journals, Offshore, vol. 70, iss. 4, p. 90. April 2010.

[53] Michigan Wheel Marine, Grand Rapids, MI, Michigan Wheel Web site [Online], Available: http://www.miwheel.com [Accessed: July 2010].

[54] F. White, Fluid Mechanics, McGraw-Hill, Inc., 1979.

[55] Murdoc Online, "NAVOCEANO Seahorse Picture" [Online], Available: http://www.murdoconline.net [Accessed: July 2010].

[56]   M. Merrill, "Existing operational unmanned systems as mobile networked nodes," Marine Technology Journal, December 2007.

[57]   B. Allen, T. Austin, N. Forrester, R. Goldsborough, A. Kukulya, G. Packard, M. Purcell and R. Stokey, "Autonomous Docking Demonstrations with Enhanced REMUS Technology," IEEE Oceans 2006 Conference Proceedings; Woods Hole Oceanographic Institution.

INITIAL DISTRIBUTION LIST

1. Defense Technical Information Center
    Ft. Belvoir, Virginia

2. Dudley Knox Library
    Naval Postgraduate School
    Monterey, California

www.ingramcontent.com/pod-product-compliance
Lightning Source LLC
Chambersburg PA
CBHW050617110426
42813CB00008B/2594